Crisis Management & Public Policy

Singapore's Approach to Economic Resilience

Singapore's Approach to Economic Resilience

Crisis Management & Public Policy

Editors

Sng Hui Ying

Chia Wai Mun

School of Humanities & Social Sciences,
Nanyang Technological University, Singapore

World Scientific

NEW JERSEY • LONDON • SINGAPORE • BEIJING • SHANGHAI • HONG KONG • TAIPEI • CHENNAI

Published by

World Scientific Publishing Co. Pte. Ltd.
5 Toh Tuck Link, Singapore 596224
USA office: 27 Warren Street, Suite 401-402, Hackensack, NJ 07601
UK office: 57 Shelton Street, Covent Garden, London WC2H 9HE

Library of Congress Cataloging-in-Publication Data
Crisis management and public policy : Singapore's approach to economic resilience / edited by Hui Ying Sng & Wai Mun Chia.
p. cm.
Includes bibliographical references and index.
Summary: "One of the key themes of this book is to study economic crises and financial crises, and the policy measures that are available to manage them. The second key theme of the book is to review several public policies in Singapore, such as competition, healthcare, training, free trade agreements, state capitalism and inequality."--Publisher's description.
ISBN-13: 978-981-4340-89-2
ISBN-10: 981-4340-89-8
1. Singapore--Economic policy. 2. Crisis management--Singapore. 3. Financial crises--Singapore. I. Sng, Hui Ying. II. Chia, Wai Mun.
HC445.8C75 2011
339.5095957--dc22

2011017556

British Library Cataloguing-in-Publication Data
A catalogue record for this book is available from the British Library.

Typeset by Stallion Press
Email: enquiries@stallionpress.com

Printed in Singapore by World Scientific Printers.

CONTENTS

FOREWORD

In 1965, the year of Independence, Singapore's GDP per capita of US$512 was lower than that of Jamaica, South Africa, Chile and Uruguay. In 2009, Singapore's GDP per capita of US$36,534 was higher than the United Kingdom's, Italy's and New Zealand's. Furthermore, this was achieved on the back of full employment, healthy fiscal budget balances, growing foreign exchange reserves, low inflation rate, and significant progress in various social areas such as housing, education, and health.

However, in the 45 years since Independence, Singapore has weathered as many as five economic/financial crises. Through timely implementation of appropriate policy measures and cooperation among the tripartite partners (government, employers and workers), Singapore has emerged from these crises swiftly and stronger than before. The same cannot be said of quite a number of developing countries whose growth was derailed after a financial or economic crisis.

What are the factors that have propelled Singapore's growth and development? What are the factors that have contributed to the resilience of the Singapore's economy? I would say that it is a combination of good governance, heavy investment in human, physical and social capital, trade openness and free-market orientation. I would also say that it is the permeation of good economic thinking in the socio-economic policy making process.

As Singapore enters the 21st century, economic uncertainty on the global front looks set to worsen — debt crises in the developed nations, asset bubbles in the developing nations, and fluctuating commodity prices. All these would have huge impacts on the Singapore economy.

What are the policy choices we have when confronted with future external crises? How can we fine-tune our policies on competition, healthcare, training, Free Trade Agreements, or state capitalism to build a more resilient economy? These are some of the issues that are discussed in depth in this book. We hope that through the active discussions presented in this book, there will be greater clarity in our understanding of the various economic policies and issues.

September 2010

Euston Quah
Professor of Economics
Co-Director, Economic Growth Centre
Editor, Singapore Economic Review
Acting Chair, School of Humanities
and Social Sciences
Nanyang Technological University
Singapore

CONTRIBUTORS

Sarah CHAN

Sarah Chan is a senior economist at the Monetary Authority of Singapore. Prior to joining the central bank, she was a researcher at the Nanyang Technological University (NTU) as well as the East Asian Institute where she penned a number of papers and articles for publication. Some of her works have appeared in international peer-reviewed or refereed journals including the *Asian Survey*, *Asia Pacific Business Review*, *East Asia: An International Quarterly*, and *China: An International Journal*. Her research interests include East Asian economic development, regional trade and investment, as well as econometric modeling. She has a Master's degree in applied economics from the National University of Singapore and is currently pursuing doctoral studies at NTU.

CHEE Yoke Heong

Chee Yoke Heong is a researcher with the Third World Network in Malaysia and a freelance writer. She was a winner of the Developing Asia Journalism Award under the auspices of the Asian Development Bank Institute in 2005 and 2009. She was also a fellow of the Asia Journalism Fellowship at the Nanyang Technological University (NTU) in Singapore in 2010. Her contribution in this book is the result of the research conducted during her three-month stint at NTU.

Rosalind CHEW

Associate Professor Rosalind Chew teaches Labour Economics and Labour Relations in the Division of Economics at the Nanyang Technological University in Singapore. She received her graduate training in Economics both in Singapore (PhD, NUS) and Canada (MA and ABD, Western Ontario). She has four books to her credit, *Workers' Perceptions on Wage Determination in Singapore* (Times Academic Press), *The Singapore Worker: A Profile* (Oxford University Press), *Employment-Driven Industrial Relations Regimes* (Avebury) and *Wage Policies in Singapore: A Key to Competitiveness* (International Labour Organisation). She has also published in various journals, including *Computational Economics*, the *International Journal of Manpower*, *Review of Pacific Basin Financial Markets and Policies*, and *Journal of Enterprising Communities*. Awards she has received include the Singapore National Book Prize, 1996 and the Highly Commended Award of the Emerald Literati Network Awards for Excellence, 2009. Her research interests include industrial relations, labour markets and entrepreneurship.

CHEW Soon Beng

Chew Soon Beng is Professor of Economics and Industrial Relations at Nanyang Technological University, Singapore. He received his PhD from the University of Western Ontario, Canada. He is the author of *Small Firms in Singapore* (Oxford University Press), *Trade Unionism in Singapore* (McGraw Hill), *Employment-Driven Industrial Relations Regimes* (Avebury), *Values and Lifestyles of Young Singaporeans* (Prentice-Hall), and *Foreign Enterprises in China: Operation and Management* (in Chinese). He has also published in journals such as the *Singapore Economic Review*, the *China Economic Review*, *Review of Pacific Basin Financial Markets and Policies*, the *Journal of Advances in Pacific Basin Business Economic and Finance*, and *International Journal of Business and Globalisation*. His current research interests include trade unionism, labour markets analysis, globalisation and entrepreneurship.

CHIA Wai Mun

Chia Wai Mun obtained her Bachelor's degree in Economics from the University of London with First Class Honours in 1996. She was then awarded the Datuk Paduka Hajjah Saleha Ali Academic Outstanding Award for her exceptional academic performance at international level in 1997. In 1998, with the support of the London School of Economics (LSE) Scholarship, she pursued her Master's degree at LSE. In 2006, she graduated with a PhD degree from NTU. She is currently Assistant Professor at the Division of Economics, NTU. Prior to joining NTU, she was an industry analyst at the Federation of Malaysian Manufacturers. Her current research interests are international macroeconomics, economic integration in East Asia and cost-benefit analysis. She is an assistant editor for the *Singapore Economic Review*. She is also a research consultant for the ASEAN Secretariat working on managing net foreign assets in Asia. She has published widely in internationally reputable journals such as *Economic Record* and *Journal of Economic Dynamics and Control*.

HO Kong Weng

Dr. Ho Kong Weng obtained his PhD from the University of Chicago. He has been teaching HE405 Growth Theory and Empirics and HE192 Economic Theory at the Nanyang Technological University. Currently he is supervising two graduate students and five undergraduates in their theses. He has mentored JC/IP students under the Nanyang Research Program (NRP) and his students had won a Merit Award and four Gold Awards. Dr. Ho has published in the areas of social mobility, international outsourcing, wage inequality, technopreneurship, and unemployment, including both theoretical investigations and empirical studies using Singapore data. His current research topics include intergenerational transmission of religious human capital, economic growth of a small open economy in a world of ideas, trade and indeterminacy, non-monotonic relationship between human capital and unemployment, and happiness studies. He has provided consulting services to government agencies on projects related to incarceration, social attitudes and well-being, youth research, and evaluation of work support programmes in Singapore. Dr. Ho is happily married to Soo Phin; their six-year-old Raymond and four-year-old Yohann are blessings from the Lord.

LAM Chuan Leong

Mr. Chuan-Leong Lam is Ambassador at Large with the Ministry of Foreign Affairs and is the Chairman of the Competition Commission of Singapore. Mr. Lam retired in 2006 after serving as the Permanent Secretary of the Ministries of Finance, the Environment, National Development, Trade and Industry, and Communications and Information. Prior to that, he was the Principal Private Secretary to former Prime Minister, Mr. Lee Kuan Yew. He also served with the Ministry of Defence as a Deputy Secretary. He also served as Chairman of the Infocomm Development Authority and the National Science and Technology Board, now renamed as A*Star. He was a board member of the Monetary Authority of Singapore, the *de facto* central bank in Singapore. He has served on the boards of several Singapore companies.

Mr. Lam's key areas of interest and expertise are in the application of complexity science, behavioural and cognitive science to general management and microeconomic issues. During his stint at the Ministry of Trade and Industry, he took an active part in the formation of the Asia Pacific Economic Community (APEC), the Suzhou project, the Vehicle Quota System, the liberalisation of the telecommunications and energy sectors, as well as trade and science and technology policies. He was involved in the formulation of general competition policy, regulation of the telecommunications sector, privatisation of government services and in the policy and use of Public Private Partnership in Singapore.

LIM Chong Yah

Professor Lim Chong Yah was the founding Head of the Division of Applied Economics, at the University of Malaya in Kuala

Lumpur, prior to becoming the Head of the Department of Economics and Statistics (1977–1992) and the Dean of the Faculty of Arts and Social Sciences (1971–1977) at the National University of Singapore. He is currently the Albert Winsemius Chair Professor of Economics and the Director of the Economic Growth Centre at the Nanyang Technological University. Some of his long list of academic publications have been translated into Chinese, Japanese and Malay. One has been translated into Braille. Professor Lim was the President of the Economic Society of Singapore for 18 years and for 13 years (1978–1991), the Editor of the *Singapore Economic Review*. For his important contributions to scholarship and education, Soka University of Japan conferred on him the "Doctor Honoris Causa" in 1995, and three years later the Soka Gakkai International, Japan awarded him with the "Chubu Award of Highest Glory". Hainan University awarded him an Honorary Professorship and the Hainan Provincial Government made him Honorary Chairman of the Hainan University Council. Indiana University in the US conferred on him the John W. Ryan Alumni Award for "Distinguished Contributions to International Education". Professor Lim, however, is more than just a distinguished scholar, an eminent educator and an internationally well known development economist. In 1987, the Ikatan Sarjana Ekonomi Indonesia conferred on him in Bali, the Distinguished Award for founding the Federation of ASEAN Economic Associations. For his important contributions to economic and national development of Singapore and its trade union movement as founding Chairman of the tripartite National Wages Council (1972–2001) and founding Chairman of the Skills Development Fund (SDF), the National Trades Union Congress conferred on him the Meritorious Service Award in 1985 and the Distinguished Service Award in 1999. The Singapore Government awarded him with the Public Service Star (BBM) on Singapore's National Day in 1976, the Meritorious Service Medal (PJG) in 1983 and the Distinguished Service Order (DUBC) in 2000. For his distinguished services to the university and society, in 2001, the NUS established a Lim Chong Yah Professorship at the Faculty of Arts and Social Sciences, where he was Dean, in his honour.

SNG Hui Ying

Sng Hui Ying is Research Associate in the School of Humanities and Social Science at the Nanyang Technological University (NTU). From 2000 to June 2010, she was Lecturer of Economics at NTU. She obtained her PhD (Economics) from NTU and her B.SocSci. (Hons) and M.SocSci. (Applied Economics) from the National University of Singapore. She was awarded the Lim Chong Yah Book Prize for being the best candidate completing the Masters Degree course. Her research areas include development economics, Southeast Asian economies and the Singapore economy. Prior to joining NTU, she was a broadcast journalist/producer with Mediacorp News and a senior research officer with the Jurong Town Corporation. In 2002, she participated in a consultation project led by Professor Lim Chong Yah to advise the government of Mauritius on wage determination system and wage reform issues. She is the co-editor of the books *Singapore and Asia in a Globalized World: Contemporary Economic Issues and Policies* (World Scientific) and *Singapore and Asia: Impact of the Global Financial Tsunami and other Economic Issues* (World Scientific). Her research monograph, *Economic Growth and Transition: Econometric Analysis of Lim's S-Curve Hypothesis*, was published in 2010.

TAN Di Song

Tan Di Song is currently a PhD candidate at the Division of Economics at the Nanyang Technological University. He obtained his B.Sc (Economics) with First Class Honours from University College London. His research interests include labour economics, economics of the family and development economics.

TAN Kim Heng

Tan Kim Heng obtained his Bachelor of Engineering from the University of Adelaide, Master of Commerce from the University of

New South Wales and PhD in Economics from the University of Sydney. He taught economics at the University of New South Wales and Macquarie University in Australia before joining the Nanyang Technological University. His research interests are in the theoretical foundations of fiscal and monetary policies.

Linda TAN Hui Min

Linda Tan Hui Min is currently an analyst in the healthcare industry. Before joining the sector, she graduated with a Masters of Science in International Political Economy at the Nanyang Technological University; she had obtained her Bachelor of Science (with Merit) and Bachelor of Social Science (Honours) at the National University of Singapore. She was formerly an economics lecturer as well as a recipient of the Public Service Commission Teaching Scholarship.

Walter Edgar THESEIRA

Walter Theseira is an applied empirical microeconomist who has written on topics in public and labour economics, and industrial organization. His research has explored the causes of international social security reform, the effects of market competition on racial discrimination in credit markets, and the effects of social capital on local volunteer firefighting departments in the United States. His research has been selected for presentation at prestigious international conferences including the Trans-Atlantic Doctoral Conference at the London Business School, and the 2010 American Economic Association Annual Meeting. In conjunction with his research on international social security issues, he has served as a short-term consultant with the World Bank's Social Protection Team. His previous applied economic policy consulting experience includes evaluating the economic feasibility of nuclear power in US energy policy as part of a research team at the University of Chicago. Currently, with the support of a grant from NTU, he is expanding his research on volunteerism and social capital to explore how public financing affects private contributions to public goods. He is actively seeking opportunities to contribute to applied economic and social policy in Singapore via collaboration with other researchers and government bodies. After completing his PhD in Managerial Science and Applied Economics from the Wharton School of the University of Pennsylvania, Walter Theseira joined NTU in 2009 as an Assistant Professor in the Division of Economics.

Part 1

Economic Crisis Management

Chapter 1

THE NATIONAL WAGES COUNCIL (NWC) AND MACROECONOMIC MANAGEMENT IN SINGAPORE

LIM Chong Yah

In the 29 years as the Chairman of the National Wages Council (NWC), Professor Lim Chong Yah participated in the macroeconomic management of one inflationary crisis and two recessionary crises in Singapore. This chapter describes the NWC's involvement in Singapore's management of the 1974 fuel and food crisis and the 1998 Asian Financial Crisis, and the totally opposite but equally effective wage policies employed during the two crises. Also explained, are the principles and arrangement of the NWC that have successfully led to harmonious, yet effective tripartism in Singapore, a flexible wage system, industrial peace, and a comprehensive programme of training and retraining of workers.

FIVE CRISES

For a period of 45 years since independence in 1965, the Singapore economy grew by an average rate of about 7.8% per annum. This growth rate is very high indeed by any standard. But what is not very well known is that within the four and a half decades of superlative real growth rates, the Singapore economy encountered as many as

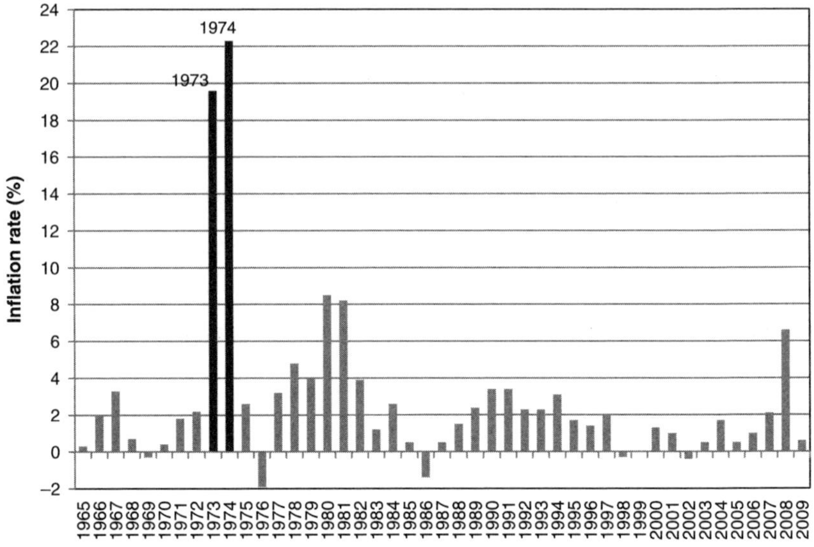

Fig. 1: Singapore inflationary years since independence.

Source: http://www.singstat.com.sg (Retrieved on 8 August 2010).

five crises, one in 1973/74, one in 1985, one in 1998, one in 2001, and one in 2009. Of which, the 1973/74 crisis was an inflationary crisis (Fig. 1), while the rest were recessionary crises (Fig. 2).

NATIONAL WAGES COUNCIL

In this chapter, I focus only on two of the crises: that in 1973/74 and that in 1998. Before we go into the crisis diagnoses and prescriptions, let me first very briefly explain the National Wages Council (NWC). It is a tripartite body set-up by the Government, and it is made up of top representatives of all the three social partners, namely, the employers, the Government, and the trade unions. It was founded in February 1972 with me as the independent chairman. Without break, including at the time of the first three crises, I was its chairman. I stepped down as NWC chairman in March 2001, having served as chairman for nearly 30 years (1972–2001).

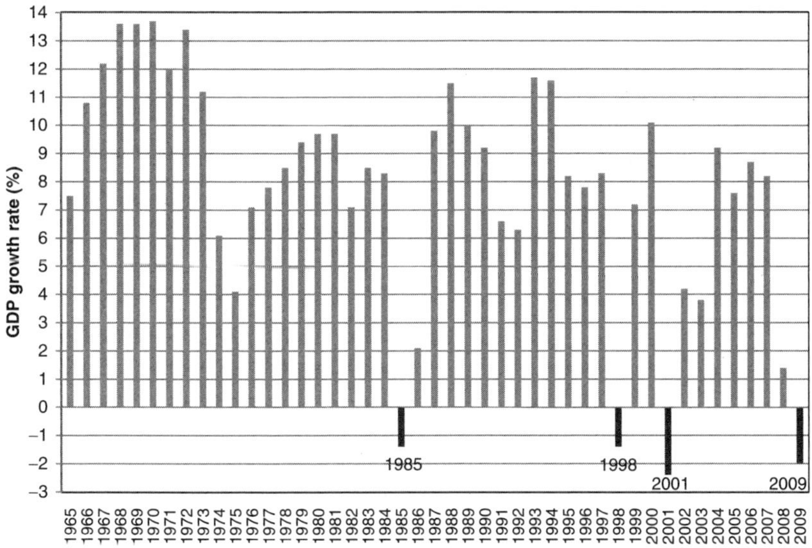

Fig. 2: Singapore recessionary years since independence.

Source: http://www.singstat.com.sg (Retrieved on 8 August 2010).

TRIPARTISM AND FLEXIBLE WAGE SYSTEM

If simple equations are to be used, the NWC is equated with not only (1) *Tripartism*, but also (2) *Flexible Wage System*. Tripartism in the NWC means decisions on changes in national wage policy, wage systems, and wage rates have to have the written public agreement of all the three social partners, all the 30 members, and alternate members of the NWC. Decision by a majority would be divisive, could become combative, and would usher in insurmountable serious implementation problems. *En passant*, the South Korean NWC failed because it carried the decision of only two of the three social partners, namely the Government and the employers. In effective tripartism, a symbiosis among the three social partners is necessary or should emerge.

First, confrontation, including confrontational bargaining, as was the mode before the NWC, has gradually been replaced by social partnership and tripartite co-operation, as without compromise and co-operation, a unanimity of votes could not be obtained.

Second, a flexible wage policy implies changing wage increase guidelines from year to year according to changing circumstances, changing macroeconomic variables, such as inflation rate, unemployment rate, unit labour cost, relative unit labour cost, return on capital, productivity growth rate, and general international competitiveness of the Singapore economy. A flexible wage system implies not just its ability to adjust wages downwards, but also upwards, in both cases without industrial discord. These yearly macroeconomic guidelines are intended for microeconomic applications at the company and the individual levels. At the company level, if both parties agree, they can deviate from the guidelines to the extent that they consider prudent. Market determinants must continue to prevail.

The Central Provident Fund (CPF) system has been an integral part of the wage system in Singapore, and at times central to the wage adjustment process. Unlike the well known traditional pension scheme, the CPF is a compulsory national individualised savings scheme. No pooling of individual contributions is involved. No inter-generational transfer of savings is involved. In short, general wage increase or decrease guidelines may have two elements: the voluntary element and the compulsory CPF component.

INDUSTRIAL HARMONY

Other than the most important sharing of the national economic cake, industrial harmony has also been high on the agenda of the NWC. During the whole period of the NWC, there has been, thank goodness, hardly any strike or any lock-out. This is in stark contrast to the earlier pre-NWC years, particularly in the 1950s and the 1960s, where strikes, or *mogok* in Malay, and 罢工 in Chinese, were the order of the day (Fig. 3).

One main reason why strikes have petered out in the NWC years was the introduction by the NWC of the right for *unilateral* reference to a neutral third party for non-legally binding conciliation, and if this fails, to the Arbitration Court for legally binding settlement (Lim, 1974). Prior to this, consent of both parties was required. The second reason is that conciliatory bodies and the Arbitration Court

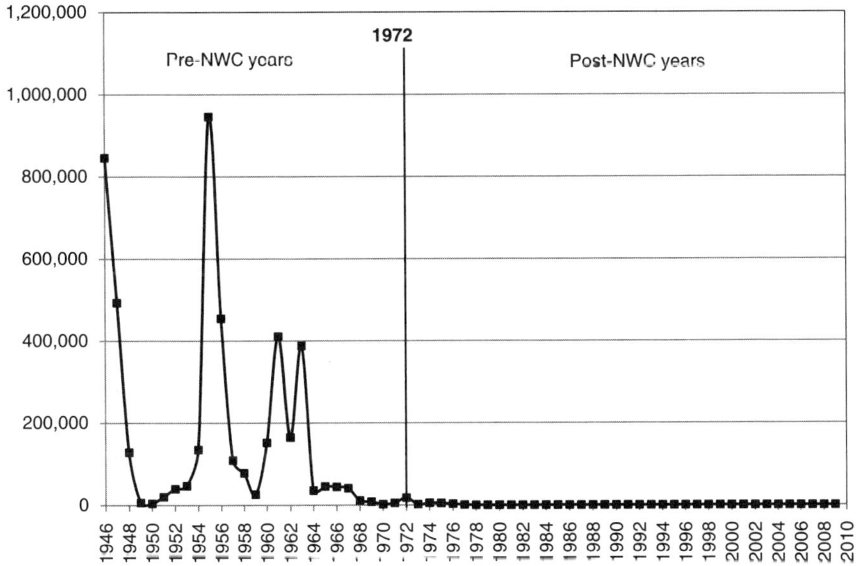

Fig. 3: Industrial relations (man-day lost in strikes, 1946–2009).

Source: Ministry of Manpower

should "take cognisance" of the recommended guidelines of the NWC in their deliberation. Prior to the setting up of the NWC, no wage guideline was available. The guidelines of NWC, on the other hand, were published in the Gazette. So, if simple equations were to be used, NWC should be closely equated or associated with, not only (1) Tripartism and (2) Wage Flexibility but also (3) *Industrial Peace and Harmony*.

TRAINING AND RETRAINING

And yet, the NWC functional picture is still not complete. The NWC was also closely associated with initiating and propagating the training of workers as an integral part of the general wage and cost increase. In 1979, the Skills Development Fund (SDF), a product of the NWC, came into being. The tripartite SDF was allotted (in 1980) as much as 4% of the workers' wage as compulsory contribution for workers' training and retraining (Lim, 1979). I was appointed as the Fund's founding chairman. I took it also as a part of my public service function, since I was too old to do National Service. So, strictly, the simple NWC equation should also include (4) NWC = *Workers' Training and Retraining.*

THE FIRST CRISIS

The NWC background stage is now more or less set for a more meaningful discussion of the first economic crisis faced by Singapore after independence in 1965. In 1971, the USA, cumbered with "persistent fundamental disequilibrium" in the balance of payments, was forced to abandon the international gold exchange standard, then fixed at US$35 to a fine ounce of gold. There was simply not enough gold left at Fort Knox to meet increasing global demand as a global currency backing medium of last resort. The global exchange rate system soon lapsed into turmoil. Most countries, in going off gold, opted for the floating system, with different degrees of managed floating. Inflationary pressures in the US were so strong that what was to be known as monetarism led by Milton Friedman was, rightly, the most popular suggested cure. The then popular Philips' Curve was discarded. Monetarism replaced Keynesianism. Monetarism meant the serious curb on money supply, the increase of which was used to finance increasing serious US budget deficits. At that time, the deficit financing was internal, not external as in the later Bush and Obama years.

The Organisation of Petroleum Exporting Countries (OPEC) went into action. In 1973 and 1974, it raised the price of petroleum gas fourfold, from US$2.8 per barrel in 1973 to US$10.4 per barrel in 1974. The initial demand–pull inflation in the USA soon became cost–push inflation for petroleum-importing economies outside the USA, like what came to pass in Singapore then. Many countries found it difficult to adjust to this mounting global stagflation crisis. Mass protests on inability to cope with the rising costs of living could even find their way to the then very much stable safe-haven British Colony of Hong Kong. Large-scale strikes and mass protests also took place in the then much admired fast advancing West German economy. The protest in West Germany had its roots in the unwillingness of employers to rewrite their five-year wage contracts in the face of unexpected serious global price inflation.

NWC RESPONSE

How should we react in Singapore? The external shock in Singapore took the form of imported high inflation with real threats of serious rising unemployment. The misery index, then a measure much in vogue, meaning a combination of the inflation index and the unemployment index, was mounting. Singapore then too had three- or five-year wage agreement contracts. Singapore too witnessed global rising fuel and food costs, threatening the fabric of our society. Thank goodness, the NWC had been born two years earlier. The NWC in early 1974 at an emergency meeting initiated by the Government recommended a general wage increase of S$25 as an interim measure. Since pay then was very low and the per capita income of Singapore too was very low, the S$25 was a big sum of money to both employers and workers. The anti-dote worked. The NWC was given a little more time to work out the final wage increase guideline.

In May 1974, the wage increase of S$40 + 6% net was recommended to the Singapore Government by the NWC (Lim, 1974). The Government accepted it for implementation without delay. This was the first serious attempt at the introduction of a flexible wage policy in Singapore. All members of the NWC signed the memorandum, meaning the recommendation had the unanimous support of all members of the NWC, including all the employers' representatives. The word *net* is important. It meant over and above the built-in wage increase in the collective wage agreements. The sanctity of the contract law was thus not violated. The dollar quantum of S$40 was meant to benefit more the lower income workers. The formula was inclusive of the S$25 interim recommendation. The average built-in wage increase was then about 4% in collective agreements. The total wage increase was thus S$40 + 10%. The total wage increase came to about 25% of general wages. That at that time was to most Singaporean a very unexpected enormous wage increase recommendation. The NWC, however, noted that the monthly inflation rates at that time were running at about 30% (Lim, 1975). Though the then popular mechanical wage-indexation practice elsewhere could not find any support within the NWC, inflation rate was not ignored in our deliberation.

As stated, the public in Singapore did not expect such a huge wage increase. It was completely unexpected, but it was most welcome by the trade unions and all the workers in Singapore. Remaining doubts about the NWC as an instrument to suppress wages were, to use a Marxist expression, thrown to the dustbin of history. Confidence in the credibility, impartiality, and integrity of the NWC rose to the highest level. The NWC, however, carried the clear warning that it would recommend a wage freeze or wage cut should the situation warrant it in the future and urged everyone to put their shoulders to the wheel to raise productivity of the individuals, of the firms, and of the country to ensure that our economy remained competitive.

Since the enormous wage increase would swell up the domestic income stream and increase the already high inflationary pressures, the NWC also recommended that an important part of the increase should take the form of an increase in the CPF contribution by raising the employers' compulsory contribution rate further from 11% to 15% of wages.

As NWC recommendations are not mandatory or legally binding so that the market mechanism could remain intact, the unanimity principle and the endorsement by the Government were critical in implementation by the three social partners. The Government, in its wisdom, set the motion going by taking the lead in implementation for all its employees including those in statutory boards. The unionised private sector followed suit. The acceptance of the recommendation became very widespread. But small business units who could not or would not implement the total wage increase guideline had still to pay the compulsory CPF wage increase element to their employees.

As expected, the package of the wage increase guideline contributed greatly to diminish potential public unrest, which came to pass, in, say, even Hong Kong and West Germany. A post-mortem carried out later by the NWC showed the success of the new flexible wage system to meet the unexpected external shock. The marginal efficacy of capital, as expected, went up a great deal with the wage increase mix. This was partly a consequence of money illusion. Real profit margin was not as high as the nominal rise in profit. The CPI index in 1975 went down to 2.6% and stayed down at very low levels in subsequent years. The CPI in fact went down to –1.9% in 1976. Stagflation, the global scourge at that time, was completely in check in Singapore. Real GDP rate was maintained at 6.1% in 1974 and went up to nearly double-digit figures in subsequent years (See Table 1 in Appendix).

On reflection, should NWC then follow the monetarist policy of controlling M_1, M_2, and M_3 to bring down the rate of inflation as was then strongly advocated by Milton Friedman? For sure, the US inflation was demand-pulled. The Singapore inflation was cost-pushed, more specifically an imported inflation. The US inflation was an autonomous inflation. The US did not have an imported inflation. At that time, the US was self-sufficient in oil supply. The US exported the inflation to other economically interlinked countries through the international circular cumulative causation process. Rightly, the US sought to control the inflationary spiral through the control of the inflationary supply of money.

Algebraically, the US sought to control $\%\Delta P$ in the well-known quantity equation

$$\%\Delta M + \%\Delta V \approx \%\Delta P + \%\Delta Y$$
$$\Rightarrow \quad \%\Delta M \approx \%\Delta P, \text{ if } V \text{ and } Y \text{ remain constant}$$

through the control of $\%\Delta M$, the rate of increase in money supply.

In Singapore, in my view, the NWC rightly controlled the imported inflation through a mixed of nominal wage increase and through the increase in the compulsory CPF savings rate. In passing, I should add that this increase in compulsory savings was later developed by the

Government into an important source of finance for the purchase of public housing in Singapore.

Again on reflection, had Singapore used Keynesianism, and the Keynesian Revolution was very much in vogue then, the imported inflation would be aggravated by the Keynesian deficit financing strategy. Deficit financing would have added fuel to the fire. Besides, the foreign leakage component is too big in a very open economy like Singapore's. Thirty odd years down the road, I would still maintain that not only the NWC's diagnosis of the economic malaise was the right one, but also the prescription for the economic trouble was also the right one, including the timing, the quantum, and the nature of the wage increase.

Lastly, of particular interest in the first economic crisis after independence is that the external shock was closely associated with US twin deficits, the gold price, the oil price, the global exchange rate system, and the choice of currency reserves. The Third Crisis that I am to talk about has something to do with the US dollar and regional exchange rates but the Third Crisis was quite a different kettle of fish from the first, as we would see. Even the prescription was totally different, opposite in fact.

No exchange rate adjustment had ever been contemplated, as for a small open economy like Singapore's, exchange rate is a double-edged weapon. Besides, Singapore then was under the strict Currency Board system, where exchange rate stability was very much treasured. Neither was the NWC given the option to use the country's exchange reserves to fight the stagflation. Indeed, that remedy was out of the question, as there was hardly any reserve to talk about then. It had still to be built up.

THE THIRD CRISIS

I would now skip the 1985 crisis to go to the 1998 one, except to mention that as planned, the Skilled Development Cess recommended by the NWC in 1979 was cut from 4% of wages to 1% of wages in 1985 as an integral part of crisis management strategy. As had earlier planned and announced, the cut would be effected in a recession and was done. The 4% cess left behind with the SDF sufficient accumulated reserves for the recessionary years, where training and re-training of unemployed workers or would-be laid-off workers could be mounting. This kind of macroeconomic sequencing could only be done in an environment where functional tripartism prevails, and where the Government in particular was wise, stable, and far-sighted enough to subscribe to and implement such a policy over an uncertain cycle. Can one now wonder why the Switzerland-based International Institute for Management Development (IMD) evaluates Singapore's system of public governance and industrial relations as number one on both counts in the world?

The 1998 exchange rate crisis caught everyone by surprise. I have deliberately used 1998 instead of 1997 for Singapore, because Singapore could not be in an economic crisis in 1997 when real GDP growth rate in that year was a high of 8.3%. True, in 1997, Thailand was in a crisis, and that contagion spread to Malaysia, Indonesia, and to South Korea through the regional circular cumulative causative process in East Asia, including Singapore by 1998. The NWC, which included the Government and the trade unions, had watched the East Asian economic storm with much anxiety but adopted a "watchful waiting" policy for Singapore. The NWC did not find it absolutely necessary to react until in September 1998. That was considered the best time to deflate costs to stay competitive, and to keep the economy afloat in the midst of mounting turmoil in much of East Asia, with the collapse of many neighbouring exchange rates and their stock markets, if not their central bankers as well.

As chairman of the NWC, it was my duty to initiate action by calling for an emergency meeting of the NWC in September 1998. I went to see Dr Lee Boon Yang, who was then the Minister of Manpower. A subset of the NWC met for an early working breakfast in the Tower Club. I still remember very clearly that Mr Khaw Boon Wan, as Permanent Secretary of the Ministry of Trade and Industry, was the chief spokesman for the Government. Mr Lim Swee Say led the NTUC group and Mr Stephen Lee, as usual, was the chief spokesman of the employers. We agreed to this cost-cutting formula to be presented to the main body of the NWC. Production costs were to be cut by S$10.5 billion, roughly one-third would take the form of an employers' CPF rate cut, roughly one-third end-of-the-year variable wage component wage cut, and another one-third took the form of the cut in government fees, charges, and taxes.

Could the NWC, the Singapore Government, and the Singapore society implement such a painful wage cut policy without strong public confidence in the NWC, and in particular, in the Singapore Government? Could this be done without effective functioning tripartism? No. A resounding no. That would be impossible. You need a state with impeccable public governance to carry this difficult adjustment and reforming function effectively and without adverse public reaction as to its good judgement, ability, impartiality, and integrity.

One problem of timing surfaced though. The cut in taxes and fees could be done immediately and unilaterally by the Government. The cut in CPF employers' contribution rate too could also be implemented as soon as possible. In Chinese, this immediate impact policy is called a 一针见血 policy. In English, it refers to being able to see blood immediately after a needle pricks. Not with the year-end variable component though. For the private sector, you have to wait till the end of the year when the year-end bonuses would be trimmed. In these circumstances, the NWC accepted the public proposal by the then Secretary-General of the NTUC, Mr Lim Boon Heng, to have a new monthly variable component (MVC). But this financial provision had to be built up over the years and in good years at that. But we accepted the MVC principle and policy for future implementation and to meet future crises. The flexible wage policy thus progressed to more flexibility, but could this new incorporation better stand the test of a crisis? My reply is in the positive. Yes.

Singapore's 1998 economic crisis was very much a part of the 1997–1998 East Asian economic crises, consequent on the collapse of the East Asian exchange rates. Much has been written about the crisis. In a few subsequent otherwise authoritative studies, Singapore was not placed in the crisis category. To these outside writers, Singapore had no crisis. Only Thailand, Malaysia, Indonesia, among others in East Asia, had a crisis. I was amazed and amused. Probably, Singapore had overcome the crisis so quickly and so successfully that they thought Singapore had experienced no crisis at all.

Published Singapore official statistics show that quarterly real GDP growth rates in 1998 quickly deteriorated from 4.7% in Q1 to 0.4% in Q2 and to –1.9% in Q3 and –1.2% in Q4. The Singapore Stock Exchange, as reflected by the Straits Times Index (STI) fell by as much as 62%, from 15 February 1997 to 4 September 1998. The Korea KOSPI index fell by 65% and the Jakarta SE Composite by 65% (Lim, 2009). The increasing unemployment rate in Singapore too became a very serious concern. Resident unemployment rate jumped from 1.9% in Q3 1997 to 2.6% in Q2 1998, and then to 4.4% in Q3 1998.

As it were, soon after the draconian cost-cutting announcement by the NWC and the unequivocal endorsement by the more powerful parent bodies outside the NWC, namely the Government, the NTUC, and the various employers' groups, the GDP in Singapore reacted with an upward trend, and unemployment rate took a nosedive. Exchange rate depreciation no longer became an interesting speculation. Instead, speculation was turned to how much the share prices would go up. Company profits improved, some considerably, others have their losses lessened or erased completely. Records show that real GDP growth rates rebounded in 1999 to 7.2% and 10.1% in 2000. Quarterly growth rates were more telling, there was a continuous and remarkable upward trend (Lim, 2009).

Neither the Hong Kong wage system nor the exchange rate regime was flexible enough to react positively to the East Asian exchange rate shock. The Taiwan wage system too could not react with speed. They both, however, resorted to the ingenious policy of buying up stocks at fire-sale prices, a practice not found in economics text books and learned journal articles as an expected function of the modern state, not even a modern state in distress.

We began the discussion by claming that NWC = Tripartism and NWC also = Flexible Wage Policy. Then we added to the list by saying NWC = Industrial Peace and Harmony and NWC = Training and

Re-training of Workers. Now I think we should complete the picture by including NWC = *Economic Crisis Management.* Of course, crisis management through changes in wage policy and wage rates could not be effected without a functioning tripartism and wage flexibility one way or the other. But though tripartism was envisaged, wage flexibility and particularly crisis management were not envisaged, not when I was asked to assume the chairmanship of the NWC in February 1972. I must, however, end by reiterating that the real function of the NWC, as originally envisaged, was to bring about an upward orderly wage adjustment each year, provided real GDP was growing and was expected to continue to grow at a superlative speed. That was the growth with equity function. That function has remained the core or basic policy and strategy of the NWC, as was given in the original terms of reference by the Ministry of Labour (now Ministry of Manpower).

I will end with a Chinese proverb as food for thought. "*It is easy to get a thousand prescriptions but hard to get one single remedy.*"

REFERENCES

Lim, Chong Yah (Chr) (May 1974). *NWC Memorandum to Prime Minister.*

Lim, Chong Yah (Chr) (June 1975). *NWC Memorandum to Prime Minister.*

Lim, Chong Yah (Chr) (June 1979). *NWC Memorandum to Prime Minister.*

Lim, Chong Yah (2009). *Southeast Asia: The Long Road Ahead,* 3rd Ed. Singapore: World Scientific.

APPENDIX

Table 1: Singapore's real GDP growth (%), 2000 market prices (1961–2010).

Year	Growth	Year	Growth	Year	Growth	Year	Growth	Year	Growth
1961	8.0	1971	12.0	1981	9.7	1991	6.6	2001	–2.4
1962	7.0	1972	13.4	1982	7.1	1992	6.3	2002	4.2
1963	9.9	1973	11.2	1983	8.5	1993	11.7	2003	3.8
1964	–3.8	1974	6.1	1984	8.3	1994	11.6	2004	9.2
1965	7.5	1975	4.1	1985	–1.4	1995	8.2	2005	7.6
1966	10.8	1976	7.1	1986	2.1	1996	7.8	2006	8.7
1967	12.2	1977	7.8	1987	9.8	1997	8.3	2007	8.2
1968	13.6	1978	8.5	1988	11.5	1998	–1.4	2008	1.4
1969	13.6	1979	9.4	1989	10.0	1999	7.2	2009	–2.0
1970	13.7	1980	9.7	1990	9.2	2000	10.1	2010*	14.0
Average	9.3	Average	8.9	Average	7.5	Average	7.6	Average	5.3

* Projection by the Ministry of Trade and Industry of Singapore's 2010 growth rate is 13–15% (14 July 2010).

Source: http://www.singstat.com.sg (Retrieved on 8 August 2010).

Note: Average growth rate 1961–2009 = 7.6%.

Chapter 2

UNPREPAREDNESS IN THE GREAT RECESSION*

LIM Chong Yah and SNG Hui Ying

This chapter argues that the USA was not fiscally or otherwise prepared for the subprime crisis that degenerated into the recent global Great Recession. Different methods of financing budget deficits are then discussed, followed by an evaluation of the impact on the economy with different forms of fiscal spending, particularly on the internal and external values of money. The chapter also compares the recent unprecedented US recession with the earlier experience of Japan as well as with China and India today in terms of the composition in fiscal spending and different forms of fiscal financing. It concludes that despite the limitations of the US method of pump priming and US unpreparedness, the world would soon move out of the recession with the universal pursuit of a cheap credit monetary policy and substantial deficit in fiscal

* Special lecture given at the opening of the Singapore Economic Review Conference (SERC) 2009 on 6 August 2009 at the Swissotel, Singapore. The basic prognostication of this chapter of global recovery turns out to be correct, very correct. However, as this is a time-sensitive chapter, some detailed observations and evaluations have become inevitably somewhat outdated. The newly emerged serious debt problems of the so-called PIIGS (Portugal, Italy, Ireland, Greece, and Spain) have captured global media headlines (April 2010). These economies appear to fall into the broad picture of unpreparedness as well, not just the USA.

policy. The global stock indexes, as one of the important leading indicators, have all shown very positive upturn, particularly so outside the USA and Japan. A prognostication of the US rates of national income growth after recovery is also done against the backdrop of the S-Curve theory.

FISCAL FINANCE

When the recent economic crisis in the form of a serious unprecedented recession struck the USA, she was caught completely unprepared. The serious recession was not anticipated. No scenario planning to combat the crisis had taken place during the Bush Era. The USA was running a huge budget deficit even in the boom years. When the unprecedented recession occurred in the remaining year of the Bush Administration, a bigger, much bigger budget deficit had to be budgeted for. In other words, spending beyond her means in both the private and public sectors got the USA into the serious recession and yet, ironically and paradoxically, further and much bigger spending by the public sector had to be done to get the economy out of the serious recession.

The huge Federal budget deficit during the Bush years was financed from foreign borrowing, resulting in the tremendous increase in foreign indebtedness. And yet, further foreign financing has, under the new Obama Administration, to be carried out with much and much larger increase in foreign indebtedness. At the end of 2008, the USA's gross federal debt was 70.2% of GDP. This ratio is projected to balloon to 98% in 2010 together with a budget deficit of 8.5% of GDP (Office of Management and Budget, *The 2010 Budget*, 7 May 2009). This is, by way of contrast, not the method of financing the anti-recessionary deficit used in many an East Asian country. In China, for example, the anti-recession deficit has been financed from a small part, only a very small part, of the huge accumulated foreign reserves, which amount to more than US one trillion dollars. In Singapore, similarly, the anti-recession budget deficit was financed from a part, again also a very, very small part of the accumulated foreign reserves. In the European Union, budget deficits are not allowed by law to exceed 3% of their GDP, although the enforcement of the law has been relaxed in view of the global Great Recession. In the USA, however, during the last year of the Bush Administration, the budget deficit was 3.2% of the GDP (Office of Management and Budget, *The 2010 Budget*, 7 May 2009). In 2009, it was estimated that the deficit would escalate to 13.2% per annum (*The Economist*, 4 July 2009), which is one of the largest, if not the largest, in the world.

DIFFERENT METHODS OF FINANCING DEFICITS

There are different methods of financing a deficit and the recovery impact on the economy is different. The impact can easily be gauged from the impact on domestic inflation and on the balance of payments. In other words, the impact on the internal and external values of money would be different. Four different methods of deficit financing will be briefly discussed in the following paragraphs.

One, financing through the use of accumulated foreign reserves. This source normally includes gold and other foreign exchange reserves. The undervaluation of gold as a part of the strategic reserves by governments is quite surprising. Gold has appreciated so much in value from US$35 for a fine ounce of gold in 1971 to more than US$1000 today.

Two, increasing taxation and sales of assets. This is the most unwelcome method, as increasing taxation will aggravate the recession, and assets, such as real estate, will fetch low prices in a recession, and may be seen as akin to a fire sale. As the recession is still on, the immediate introduction of the much-needed, but less-talked-about, tax on gasoline sales in the USA is likely to increase the already relatively high costs of production and lower the international competiveness of the US economy, whatever benefits it brings in as an anti-pollution and anti-congestion measure and as an important source of revenue.

Three, borrowing from abroad or internally. Internal borrowing will jack up the interest rate. This runs counter to the anti-recession policy of having as low an interest rate as possible. A sub-set of borrowing from abroad is borrowing from the IMF. It is difficult to imagine the USA borrowing from this source, she being, inter alia, the most important contributor to the Fund.

Four, a fiduciary issue or the printing of more money. The impact can be highly inflationary and is likely to lead to a devaluation of the domestic value of money, and in the second round, a depreciation of the external value, through the well-known purchasing power parity theory process.

THE US METHOD OF DEFICIT FINANCING

Prior to the Bush years and the Greenspan Era, the deficit financing method was largely through fiduciary issues. The end result was that the USA was forced to go off the international gold standard in 1971. Monetarism was rightly advocated as the solution to the crisis. Global floating exchange regimes succeeded the demise of the international gold standard. Later, under the able Greenspan supervision, foreign borrowing was resorted to, mainly through the sales of treasuries to countries, paradoxically some very much poorer countries such as China (People's Republic of China). The foreign borrowing strategy strengthens the US exchange rate, which would be pressured to fall much more if a fiduciary issue was resorted to. Foreign borrowing, however, ushers in affluence in terms of GDP and consumption growth, much akin to a rich family living happily beyond its means on bank loans. This is a case of short-term gain leading to long-term pain. Unfortunately, this serious mountain of foreign debts has become a serious problem for the USA.

However, in the evaluation of the methods of deficit financing in the USA, one must bear in mind that the US dollar has and is still the world's most important international medium of exchange and thus also serves as the most liquid international store of value. As long as the rest of the world (ROW) is prepared to use the US dollar as the main reserve currency, it will be prepared to lend money to the USA. The international gold standard collapsed because there was a far too large quantity of US dollars in the ROW, including belligerent France at that time. Will the current US dollar suffer the same fate because of excessive US external borrowing? Will countries that have huge US dollar reserves such as China and Japan want the US dollar to fall in value, and, therefore, also precipitate a fall in value of their huge US dollar reserve stockpiles? China and Japan, among others in the ROW, have a vested interest, at least for the time being, in the value and stability of the US dollar.

FISCAL SPENDING

Public expenditure in a recession is meant to make up for the decrease in private investment spending; the serious decrease of which is the root cause of the recession. Indeed, it is not too difficult to estimate the quantum of public investment spending that will offset the loss in private investment spending. However, public investment spending has to be income and employment generating, directly or indirectly, to be of short-term and long-term benefit. It has to be in order to increase the productive capacity of the economy on the supply side. The increase in expenditure should increase and enhance the competitiveness, including the export competitiveness, of the country, particularly in the USA.

In Asian countries, such as China and India, anti-recession countervailing expenditure is usually of the employment-creation, income-earning, income-enhancing type, such as in bottleneck infrastructural development, be they roads, seaports, airports, irrigation facilities, dams, forest rejuvenation, or school and hospital buildings and facilities. In the USA, no large-scale infrastructural development has been announced. In part, this is due to the fact that such infrastructural facilities had already been built prior to the Great Recession. However, even the much-talked-about President Obama's infrastructural rejuvenation and employment creation programmes appear to have taken on a deep back seat. In part, the approach in the USA is very short-term, for infrastructural development or rejuvenation requires time-consuming long-term planning and coordination. They are neither just "shovel ready" projects nor should they be "*roads leading to nowhere*". Bottleneck public sector infrastructural economic and social developments should complement and support the private sector activities, not supplant them or postpone the demise of private sector marginal firms or those on life support even prior to the Great Recession. Much of the deficit financing in the USA is used to bail out overstretched and debt-ridden credit institutions and the very high-cost automobile industry.

On 4 July 2009, *The Straits Times* headlines read, "India to Pour Billions into Upgrading Infrastructure". The budget, it continues in a sub-headline, is "likely to give priority to fixing roads, ports and railways and boosting power supply". In the five years to March 2012, India plans to spend, according to the Government of India Planning Commission:

> US$167 billion on power generation,
> US$79 billion on highways and bridges,
> US$65 billion on telecommunications,
> US$65 billion on railways,
> US$63 billion on irrigation,
> US$22 billion on ports,
> US$8 billion on airports.
>
> — The Straits Times (4 July 2009)

In other words, in India counter-recessionary expenditure has also resulted in the acceleration or telescoping of development spending. This is also the same *modus operandi* on bottleneck capital development in China, the other and earlier emerging giant in Asia. In China, a 4 trillion yuan (about US$570 billion) stimulus package announced in September 2008 would be spent over the next two years to finance programmes in 10 major areas, such as low-income housing, rural infrastructure, water, electricity, transportation, environment, technological innovation, and rebuilding from several disasters, most notably the 12 May 2008 Sichuan earthquake. Besides, what is not commonly known is that fiscal deficits in the USA have to be incurred at the Federal level. At the state and city levels, fiscal balance has to be, by law, maintained. In a recession with state governments' and city administrations' revenues automatically falling, the extra Federal spending may be offset by the fall in state government and city council spending. Again, this kind of fiscal arrangement appears to be another facet of US unpreparedness in confronting a disastrous economic meltdown. Asian governments, such as those in China and India, whilst having other problems, do not have this legal bureaucratic handicap. It is no wonder that the caring and most outstanding American economist, Professor Paul Krugman, has recently advocated another huge Federal stimulus package to counter the shortfall in state and city council spending (*The Business Times*, 4–5 July 2009). Krugman's advocacy is made despite the reservations in some quarters, mainly by the Republicans, of fear of runaway inflation rearing its ugly head with the present stimulus package alone.

Actually, the fear of a serious inflation in the USA under the present circumstances of a rising unemployment rate (at an unprecedented level of 9.5%) and falling prices (deflation) is rather premature. Whether the Great Recession has reached the bottom is debatable. Some encouraging green shoots may not stay green, but may wither. The USA, however, cannot put the cart before the horse. She must get out of the serious recession first before worrying about inflation. However, with US Federal expenditure not concentrating on infrastructural development and infrastructural rejuvenation as well as other income-generating long-term gestation period assets, two other legitimate problems can emerge in the not-too-distant future. One is stagflation; that is inflation with high unemployment. Another is pressure on the external value of the US dollar, through more serious deficit on current account balance, consequent on a high propensity for consumption and greater volume of imports.

Stagflation and a weakening US dollar is detrimental not only to the USA but to the entire world economy. One must bear in mind that the USA is still by far the largest economy in the world, larger than Japan, China, Germany, and Great Britain combined. However, if the US dollar collapses, a different and more troublesome global scenario would emerge. The IMF would be helpless if this occurs and unable to do anything besides advocating orderly exchange rate adjustments. How would the overvalued US dollar be adjusted to the aggravated new situation?

JAPAN AND USA COMPARISON

The stock indicators in Appendix 1 show that the two very big and troubled economies in the current global recession are the USA and Japan. Both share a number of characteristics in common. Firstly, both are very well-developed and have enjoyed very high per capita income for decades. Secondly, the recessions in both economies started off with the burst of a huge property bubble, with Japan's (starting *circa* 1989 to this day) occurring about 20 years ahead of the USA's (beginning with the subprime mortgage crisis *circa* 2008). Both used the lowering of the interest rate to contain the crisis at first, but were unsuccessful and ended up with the liquidity trap problem. The problem and the recession were to be solved through still massive fiscal stimulus, with one more very clear unpreparedness in both — both had huge fiscal deficits to begin with, at the time when their property bubbles burst. However, Japan started with and continues to have a current account surplus, whereas the USA, by way of contrast, has been running a serious deficit. Thus, the USA has to depend on further external borrowing to finance the deepening budget deficit, estimated by *The Economist* to be 13.2% of the GDP in 2009. Could the unpreparedness of both Japan and the USA in their lack of prevention and appropriate intervention for the recession imply that the US recession will be as prolonged as Japan's? The answer depends partly on the magnitude and composition of the intervention and on the speed and magnitude of recovery in the ROW. Japan's slow growth of 1–3% could be considered as a recovery, the superlative growth rate of 10% or more from the 1950s to the 1970s is no longer attainable as Japan is now a matured economy (Lim, 2005; Sng, 2010). The US deficit funding problem has yet to be really solved. One way of solving it is to let the US exchange rate continue to fall through a low interest rate policy while other countries raise their interest rates. Japan started off with a short-term Keynesian recession problem and ended up with a long-term Schumpeterian one. The USA, most unfortunately, also appears to be on this track.

THE LEADING INDICATOR

The stock market is often considered a leading indicator, though by no means a perfectly reliable one, for economic forecasting. Appendix 1 shows that if we compare the end of December 2008 stock indexes with the end of June 2009 indexes, which have just become available, the only negative index on the long list of countries is the US Wall Street DJIA (−3.1%), as against all the positive, some very positive, indexes in the ROW: China, (+64.9%), Canada (24.1%), Greece (+27.3%), Denmark (23.7%), Norway (+38.1%), Russia (+54.8%), Turkey (+40.4%), Hong Kong (+27.7%), India (54.4%), Indonesia (62.6%), and Singapore (+33.3%) (*The Economist*, 4th July 2009).

Perhaps, we should rephrase the title of this chapter: "Unpreparedness in the Great Recession in the USA" instead of just "Unpreparedness in the Great Recession". Perhaps too when we debate about decoupling, we should also talk about the sad truth of decoupling of the USA and Japan *vis-à-vis* the rest of the Asia-Pacific region rather than just decoupling of the USA with the ROW. However, in a globalised world, when G1 or G2 are in trouble, will not G7, G8, and G20 also be in trouble, though perhaps not to the same extent? The Triple C theory states that all will be in trouble through the downward circular cumulative causation process (Lim, 2001, 2009).

Fortunately, every government in the world is fighting the recession by adopting a cheap credit policy and a big budget deficit. All governments today, at the beginning of the 21st century, are much more economically savvy than they were in the 1930s. The budget deficits of 40 countries are given in Appendix 2. Countries such as Singapore, South Korea, Australia, Saudi Arabia, and China, which are more often associated with budget surplus, are all raking up substantial budget deficit this year.[1] China, India, Korea, Malaysia, Thailand, Singapore, and the Philippines have all rolled out stimulus packages that include spending on economic and social infrastructures and programmes. To assess the effect of fiscal stimulus packages on selected economies, *Oxford Economics* ran a simulation using its global macroeconomic model that treats government spending exogenously (Asian Development Bank (ADB), 2009). The simulation shows that the stimulus packages would increase the GDP of the selected Asian countries in 2009 by 0.5–6.5% points (Table 1).

With the outbreak of the US subprime mortgage in the second half of 2007 and as the global financial crisis unfolded in 2008, central banks all over the world have substantially eased their credit and monetary policies. In the USA, the target Federal Fund rate was

Table 1: Impact of fiscal stimulus packages in selected Asian economies (simulation).

		Impact on GDP (% change from baseline)		
Economy	Package as share of 2009 GDP (%)	2009	2010	2011
China	1.2	1.3	2.0	1.5
Hong Kong	1.4	1.1	0.5	0.3
India	1.6	0.5	0.3	0.3
Indonesia	1.3	1.3	0.8	0.4
Korea	2.5	1.6	1.2	1.0
Malaysia	2.6	3.1	4.1	1.5
Philippines, the	4.1	2.4	3.5	1.7
Singapore	5.9	3.6	2.8	0.4
Taiwan	2.1	1.4	1.2	0.7
Thailand	6.4	6.5	7.9	7.4

Source: ADB, 2009.

[1] In 2007, Singapore's budget surplus was 3.3% of GDP, South Korea's was 3.5%, Australia's was 1.6%, Saudi Arabia's was 12.3%, and China's was 0.6% (Economist Intelligence Unit, 2009).

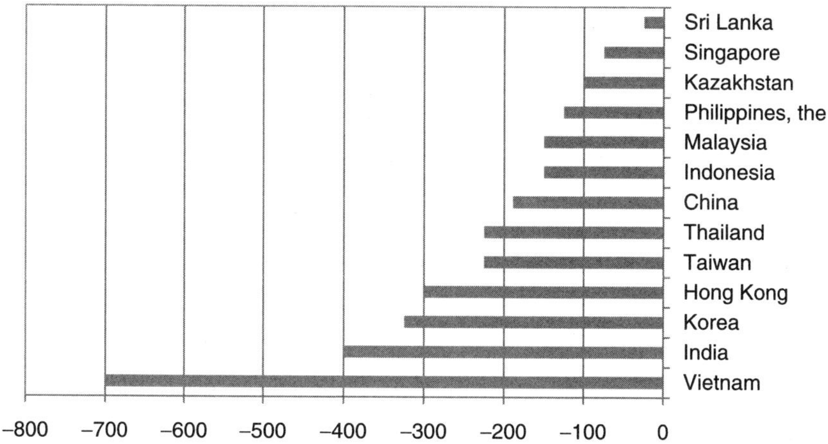

Fig. 1: Change in policy rates from 30 September 2008 to 16 March 2009.
Source: ADB, 2009.

repeatedly lowered from 5.25% in September 2007 to the current 0–0.5%. The European Central Bank has also cut the main European base rate from 4.25% in July 2008 to an all-time low of just 1% in May 2009. Figure 1 shows the change in the policy rates of selected Asian economies from September 2008 to March 2009. The latest low interest rates of countries are given in Appendix 3.

With the two twin attacks of expansionary fiscal policy and loose monetary policy, one should not be surprised that 2010 is forecasted to see positive growth rates in nearly all countries, including the USA with a good positive rate of +1.6%, Japan's +0.8%, as against Indonesia's +3.1%, India's +6.4%, China's +7.3%, Egypt's +3.8%, Saudi Arabia's 3.1%, and South Africa's +3.1% (*The Economist*, 4 July 2009).

In other words, beyond 2010 into the further future horizon, the long-term slow growth problem of the US economy will re-emerge, although 2011 and perhaps also 2012 will see her short-term serious recession problem solved through massive public deficit spending and an easy credit policy, with threatening inflationary pressures through more expensive imports and the continued fall in the US dollar.

THE FURTHER ROAD AHEAD

After global recovery, not necessarily at the same rate for every country, what will be the growth rate of the USA? Is there a theoretical framework for such an analysis, such a prognostication? In our view, the Trinity Growth Theory (TGT) is helpful. The theory (Lim, 2010a,b) postulates that for well-developed and mature economies, growth rates based on the existing growth parameters and connectivity can and will exhibit slow growth of 1–4%, with the more dynamic and more innovative ones taking the upper end and the less dynamic and innovative brethrens the lower end. Japan, most unfortunately, has fallen into this pattern of slow growth, at the lower end, after the bubble burst in 1989. Will the USA with a much more resourceful, a more innovative, and a more open economy in terms of talent absorption from abroad, fall into the same situation as the Japanese in the past two decades? In our view, the USA will probably take the upper road and will end up with an average of about 3% slow growth. As TGT also postulates, this implies the convergence of other emerging economies such as China, India, Vietnam, Indonesia, Malaysia, and Singapore with most probable corresponding growth rates of 6–12% per annum. The dice is cast in favour of the spread of global wealth. Is this to be feared? That depends on the perspective that one takes. This is a much welcome global development, in our view, from the global perspective and from the viewpoint of emerging economies.

REFERENCES

Asian Development Bank (2009). Asian Development Outlook 2009: Rebalancing Asia's Growth.

Economist Intelligence Unit (2009). Country Report, various countries.

Lim, Chong Yah (2001). The trinity growth theory: The ascendancy of Asia and the decline of the West. In *Economic Essays by Lim Chong Yah*, DH Hooi and AT Koh (eds.). Singapore: World Scientific.

Lim, Chong Yah (2005). Economic theory and the east Asian region. *Singapore Economic Review (Special 50th Anniversary Issue)*, 50, 495–512.

Lim, Chong Yah (2009). Trinity development model and Southeast Asian development. In *Southeast Asia: The Long Road Ahead,* 3rd Ed. Singapore: World Scientific.

Lim, Chong Yah (2010a). The deepening global recession and the great depression fear. In *Singapore and Asia: Impact of the Global Financial Tsunami and Other Economics Issues,* WM Chia and HY Sng (eds.), pp. 3–13. Singapore: World Scientific.

Lim, Chong Yah (2010b). Thc World Bank Spcncc Commission Rcport and the Trinity Growth Theory. *Singapore Economic Review,* 55(1), 49–58. Special Issue edited by Pradumna Rana on the Asian Economic Integration.

Sng, Hui Ying (2010). *Economic Growth and Transition: Econometric Analysis of Lim's S-Curve Hypothesis,* Economic Growth Centre Research Monograph Series, No. 1. Singapore: World Scientific.

The Financial Times, The Economist, The Business Times (Singapore), *The Straits Times* (Singapore), various issues, and MediaCorp TELETEXT, daily, pp. 210 and 220.

APPENDICES

Appendix 1: Global Stock Market Indices % Change from 31 December 2008 (in US$ terms, 1 July 2009)

United States (DJIA)	−3.1
United States (S&P 500)	+2.2
Japan (Nikkei 225)	+5.2
China (SSEA)	+64.9
Britain (FTSE 100)	+12.2
Canada (S&P TSX)	+24.1
Austria (ATX)	+24.2
Greece (Athex Comp)	+27.3
Denmark (OMXCB)	+23.7
Hungary (BUX)	+26.4
Norway (OSEAX)	+38.1
Russia (RTS, $ terms)	+54.8
Sweden (OMXS30)	+28.2
Turkey (ISE)	+40.4
Australia (ALL Ord)	+21.3
Hong Kong (Hang Seng)	+27.7
India (BSE)	+54.4
Indonesia (JSX)	+62.6
Malaysia (KLSE)	+21.0
Singapore (STI)	+33.3
South Korea (KOSPI)	+24.7
Taiwan (TWI)	+43.5
Thailand (SET)	+35.6
Argentina (MERV)	+35.6
Brazil (BVSP)	+65.8
Chile (IGPA)	+56.1
Egypt (Case 30)	+22.2
Israel (TA-100)	+40.9
Emerging Market (MSCI)	+36.3

Source: *The Economist*, 4 July 2009, p. 82.

Appendix 2: Global Budget Balances % of GDP 2009

Country	%	Country	%
The United States	−13.2	Turkey	−5.6
Japan	−6.8	Australia	−4.2
China	−3.8	Hong Kong	−4.1
Britain	−13.9	India	−7.7
Canada	−2.1	Indonesia	−3.0
Austria	−4.6	Malaysia	−7.8
Belgium	−4.8	Pakistan	−5.0
France	−6.6	Singapore	−4.1
Germany	−4.6	South Korea	−5.7
Greece	−6.5	Taiwan	−5.2
Italy	−5.2	Thailand	−5.6
The Netherlands	−4.1	Argentina	−1.2
Spain	−9.6	Chile	−3.3
Czech Republic	−4.0	Colombia	−3.4
Denmark	−2.5	Mexico	−5.4
Hungary	−3.9	Venezuela	−4.7
Poland	−4.0	Egypt	−7.1
Russia	−8.0	Israel	−6.2
Sweden	−4.7	Saudi Arabia	−5.1
Switzerland	−3.1	South Africa	−4.1

Source: *The Economist*, 4 July 2009, p. 82 (based on *The Economist* poll or *Economist Intelligent Unit* forecast).

Appendix 3: Global Interest Rates (three-month latest)

The United States	0.34
Japan	0.43
China	1.32
Britain	1.20
Canada	0.23
Euro Area	1.09
Austria	1.09
Belgium	1.10
France	1.09
Germany	1.09
Greece	1.09
Italy	1.09
The Netherlands	1.09
Spain	1.09
Sweden	0.28
Switzerland	0.40
Hong Kong	0.36
India	3.31
Singapore	0.50
South Korea	2.41
Taiwan	0.85
Israel	0.33
Saudi Arabia	0.65

Source: *The Economist*, 4 July 2009, p. 82.

Chapter 3
WHY ARE FINANCIAL CRISES SO COSTLY?

TAN Kim Heng

In this chapter, I explain the effects of financial crises on the macroeconomy in terms of the loss in output and employment and the fiscal costs of rescuing banks and financial institutions. Whereas recessions in a normal downturn typically mean a fall in gross domestic product of a few percentage points, recessions resulting from financial crises are much more serious. The objective of this chapter is to explain the reasons for this.

INTRODUCTION

A financial crisis occurs when a system-wide failure of the financial system disrupts financial intermediation to the extent that the system is incapable of channelling funds efficiently from savers to firms with productive investments and causes a sharp contraction in economic activity. Financial crises are costly for two reasons. The first is due to the tremendous loss of output and employment as an economy contracts in the wake of a financial crisis. The second is due to the fiscal costs incurred by governments when they bail out

Table 1: Fiscal costs and output losses of financial crises.

Country	Time frame	Lowest real GDP growth rate in % (year)	Fiscal cost (% of GDP)	Output loss (% of GDP)
Argentina	2001–	−10.9 (2002)		15
Mexico	1994–2000	−6.2 (1995)	19.3	10
Indonesia	1997–2002	−13.1 (1998)	55.0	39
South Korea	1997–2002	−6.7 (1998)	28.0	17
Malaysia	1997–2001	−7.4 (1998)	16.4	33
Thailand	1997–2002	−10.5 (1998)	34.8	40
Japan	1991–	0.9 (1992)	24.0	48
Finland	1991–1994	−6.3 (1991)	11.2	21
Sweden	1991–1994	−1.1 (1991)	4.0	11

Source: Caprio *et al.*, 2003.

banks that have insufficient capital and banks that are deemed too big to fail in a financial crisis.[1]

Table 1 summarises the fiscal costs and output losses of a sample of countries that suffered financial crises. For emerging market economies, the fiscal costs can be quite large. During the Asian Financial Crisis that swept through East Asia in 1997–1998, the fiscal costs range from 16.4% of gross domestic product (GDP) for Malaysia to 55.0% of GDP for Indonesia. Even though the fiscal costs are smaller for developed nations, they are not insignificant. For instance, Finland incurred a fiscal cost of 11.2% of GDP during its financial crisis in the early 1990s.

In a normal downturn of the business cycle, typically economies experience declines in their GDP of no more than a few percentage points. In a financial crisis, however, the recession that follows it is usually quite severe. Why is this so? The objective of this chapter is to

[1] Strictly, the fiscal costs of bank bailouts are transfers from the tax payers to the creditors and shareholders of the banks. However, in the absence of the bank bailouts, the affected banks will most likely fail, in which case the true costs would appear in the form of loss of output and employment.

explain why financial crises can result in deep recessions and are costly. To do this, we have to explain how and why financial crises affect economic activity. At first sight, it might be thought that the tremendous decline in wealth in the wake of a financial crisis would lead via the wealth effect to a loss of consumption spending and investment spending and hence to a loss of output and employment. While this effect is certainly present, it cannot explain the extent of the loss in output and employment. To be sure, the destruction of wealth is a key determinant of the loss of output, but this destruction works most potently via the financial system by disrupting financial intermediation. Unfortunately, the models in most macroeconomic texts[2] abstract away the role of the financial system in the macroeconomy. It is my hope that this chapter addresses this deficiency in the macroeconomics texts.

For the purpose of discussion and analysis in this chapter, I consider two types of financial crises, namely, banking crises and currency crises, i.e., exchange-rate crises.

BANKS AS FINANCIAL INTERMEDIARIES

Before considering banking crises, it is first necessary to understand how banks perform the role of financial intermediation. As a financial intermediary, a bank accepts deposits from savers and makes loans to firms for spending on productive investments and to consumers for spending on consumer durables. The modern banking system is characterised by a fractional reserve banking system. In such a system, a bank does not have to hold reserves to back up fully all the deposits put in by savers. Table 2 summarises a simplified bank balance sheet. On the left side of the balance sheet are the bank's assets while on the right side are the bank's liabilities. Assets are what are owned by the bank, while liabilities are what are owed by the bank. In the simple balance sheet, the bank owns

---

[2] These are usually texts on Macroeconomics at the intermediate level. This means that students who are taught Macroeconomics at the intermediate level would usually have no clue as to how a financial crisis can affect economic activity

Table 2: Simplified bank balance sheet.

Assets		Liabilities and net worth	
Reserves	8	Deposits	90
Loans	92	Capital	10
Total	100	Total	100

reserves and loans while it owes deposits put in by savers. The difference between assets and liabilities is capital provided by shareholders, also called the bank's net worth.

There are two unique features of banks that are worth noting. The first is that bank reserves are a small fraction of deposits. Under normal conditions, they are sufficient to allow for withdrawals as depositors do not withdraw deposits all at once. The second is that a bank's net worth or capital is a small fraction of the total assets. Again, under normal conditions when banks are operating profitably, the small amount of the capital relative to total assets is not a problem. Central banks usually spell out both reserve requirements and capital requirements. The minimum reserve requirement is to ensure that there is sufficient liquidity to meet depositor withdrawals, while the minimum capital requirement is to ensure that banks have sufficient net worth to absorb losses and maintain bank solvency. Banks will have to manage their assets and liabilities to ensure that they satisfy both the reserve and capital requirements stipulated by the central bank.[3]

Since banks make loans to firms for spending on productive investment and to consumers for spending on consumer durables, the amount of credit plays a crucial role in determining output and

[3] Although I discuss above the operation of banks as if they were commercial banks, taking in deposits from savers (read retail investors) and extending loans to firms (read small and medium enterprises), banks here should be interpreted more generally to include not only retail banks but also wholesale banks, taking in large short-term deposits from corporations and investing them in longer-term financial instruments. Hence, my analysis in this chapter applies not only to banks in emerging market economies but also to the so-called shadow banking system in the USA. For a discussion of the shadow banking system in the USA, see Gorton (2010).

employment. Now, the market for credit is subject to asymmetric information between lenders and borrowers. This means that borrowers have better information about their own credit worthiness and risks of defaulting on payments than lenders have about them. Under asymmetric information, default risks are increased in two ways. First, borrowers who have high default risks are the ones most likely to seek loans. This problem is known as adverse selection. Second, after the loans have been extended, borrowers have an incentive to engage in riskier behaviour than they otherwise would. This problem is known as moral hazard. Adverse selection and moral hazard influence the supply of credit in that, when these asymmetric information problems worsen as in a financial crisis during which default risks increase, banks as lenders will tighten the supply of credit.

Because default risks determine the supply of credit, the price mechanism (based on interest rates) does not clear the market for credit. This is because increases in interest rates increase default risks by encouraging more borrowers with higher default risks to apply for credit (the adverse selection problem) and also encouraging borrowers who have already taken out loans to engage in riskier activities to cover their higher interest payments (the moral hazard problem). Rather than increase interest rates, lenders ration credit.[4]

BANK FAILURE AND BANK RUNS

A bank will become insolvent and fail if borrowers default on loans to the extent that its capital is wiped out. To see this, suppose that the bank in Table 2 suffers loan defaults of 12 units and has to write down its assets by 12 units, resulting in the balance sheet summarised in Table 3.

As summarised in Table 3, bank capital is now the difference between 88 units of assets and 90 units of liabilities, i.e., bank capital is −2 units. With negative capital, the bank is now insolvent because its total assets of 88 units are insufficient to meet its liabilities of 90 units. The central bank or bank regulator would have to close down the insolvent bank.

---

[4] This model of credit rationing is due to Stiglitz and Weiss (1981).

Table 3: Bank balance sheet (with loan losses).

Assets		Liabilities and net worth	
Reserves	8	Deposits	90
Loans	80	Capital	–2
Total	88	Total	88

When depositors learn that their bank is insolvent, they would naturally turn up en masse to withdraw their deposits unless deposits are fully insured. We call this a run on the bank. If other depositors are afraid that their banks might become insolvent and run on them even though they are healthy, these banks would not have enough reserves to satisfy withdrawals. We say these banks are illiquid. Illiquid banks will fail if they cannot borrow reserves from other banks in the interbank market and the central bank does not extend loans to them. Usually, however, the central bank will act as the lender of last resort and extend loans to illiquid but otherwise solvent banks. The reason for bank illiquidity is maturity mismatch. Maturity mismatch occurs when a bank has short-term liabilities in the form of bank deposits that can be withdrawn at an instant's notice but long-term assets such as bank loans, which are payable over a longer term and which cannot be recalled at short notice to satisfy deposit withdrawals. Deposit withdrawals have to be met from bank reserves, which are insufficient, hence the illiquidity.

We see that banks can fail due to insolvency or illiquidity. Under full deposit insurance, bank runs are avoided and bank failure due to illiquidity will not arise, especially when the central bank as the lender of last resort can provide liquidity to banks that are unable to borrow from the interbank market.[5]

[5] In the recent US financial crisis and its contagion to the rest of the world, visible bank runs were rare because governments all over the world imposed full deposit insurance. However, silent or invisible bank runs did take place against the financial institutions in the US shadow banking system, for which the deposit insurance covered by the Federal Deposit Insurance Corporation (FDIC) and the lender-of-last-resort facility by the Federal Reserve did not apply. Many of the financial institutions of the shadow banking system were starved of incoming funds and failed.

BANKING CRISIS

Consider the following scenario. As a result of financial liberalisation or deregulation or insufficient regulation of the financial system, bank capital requirements are low and bank loans are excessive.[6] The loans are used to fund purchases of assets, driving up asset prices beyond their values determined by fundamental economic factors and creating an asset bubble.[7] When the asset bubble bursts and asset prices decline sharply, the net worth of borrowing firms and households holding these assets declines sharply. With assets valued less than the value of the loans taken out to finance the assets as a result of the asset-market crash, borrowers start to default on loans. As loan defaults accumulate, the value of assets on banks' balance sheets declines due to the bad debts, leading to a contraction of bank capital. If losses accumulate to the extent that bank capital is wiped out as summarised earlier in Table 3, the banks affected will become insolvent and fail.

A banking crisis occurs when many banks fail. If deposit insurance is absent or limited, depositors in a banking crisis will run on their banks to the point that even healthy banks become illiquid and fail.

---

[6] Although it is not the intention of this chapter to consider the causes of financial crises, very briefly financial crises are caused by excessive risk-taking that results from the failure to internalise the external costs that financial institutions, in taking risks and potentially contributing to system-wide failure of the financial system, impose upon the financial system. Hence, the excessive risks taken are due to the under-pricing of risks. This market failure can be corrected by proper regulation of the financial system. However, if the financial system is inadequately regulated or regulations in place are relaxed through financial liberalisation, the seeds of financial crises are sown. In short, market failure of the financial system interacting with regulatory failure of the system is a recipe for financial disasters. Regulatory failure in turn can be traced to the close relationship between business and government. On the influence that *Wall Street* has over the US government, see Johnson and Kwak (2010).

[7] Under the efficient market hypothesis, asset bubbles are not possible. One has to abandon this hypothesis in order to allow for the existence of asset bubbles.

IMPACT OF BANKING CRISIS ON ECONOMIC ACTIVITY

In a banking crisis, bank lending is drastically curtailed. There are three reasons for this. First, in the absence of deposit insurance or in the presence of limited deposit insurance, banks desire to hold more reserves to satisfy deposit withdrawals. Second, even if deposits are fully insured so that deposit withdrawals are not a problem, banks would still hold more reserves and curtail bank lending as default risks have increased, worsening the adverse selection and moral hazard problems. Third, with bank capital declining, banks will have to sell off assets including curtailing bank loans to pay off liabilities to satisfy minimum capital requirements. This is a process of deleveraging, which leads to further falls in asset prices that accentuate the asset market crash.

As a result of the drastic curtailment of bank lending in a banking crisis, consumers find it extremely difficult to obtain loans to purchase consumer durables and businesses find it difficult to fund business investment or even to fund their ongoing business operations. Output demand hence contracts sharply. In addition, the smaller net worth of borrowing firms and individuals due to the asset-price crash also causes investment and consumption spending to decline. This is because with their smaller net worth with which to pledge as collateral to banks to provide the latter protection against their borrowings, their ability to borrow is reduced. In short, credit limits are drastically tightened with severe adverse consequences for aggregate demand, output, and employment.[8]

If the decline in output demand due to the banking crisis is severe, as happened in the Great Depression in the 1930s, the banking crisis would be accompanied by deflation, in which unanticipated declines in the price level occur. As debt payments are fixed in nominal terms, unanticipated declines in the price level

[8] The credit market does not necessarily need to clear. The reason is that the market-clearing interest rate does not maximise the banks' expected return on loans. This is so as adverse selection would cause the market-clearing rate to attract more borrowers with bad credit risks. To prevent this problem, the banks choose to ration credit at a lower interest rate that maximises their expected return on loans.

raise the value of borrowing firms' liabilities in real terms and lower the real value of the firms' net worth. The decline in the net worth of borrowing firms decreases further their ability to borrow and exacerbates the contraction of output demand.[9]

The costs of a banking crisis therefore include loss of output, loss of employment, and costs incurred by the government to bail out banks. Governments bail out banks that are deemed too big to fail in that they are so interconnected with the financial system that their failure would lead to failure of other financial institutions. Governments also bail out major banks that have insufficient capital. Bank bailouts take the form of recapitalising the banks or buying up bad debts from the banks.

A relevant question to ask is: why cannot governments and central banks take policy actions to minimise the impact of financial crises and hence minimise the costs of financial crises? The answer is that they do. However, as experience has shown, governments and central banks are usually unprepared for financial crises so that, by the time the policy makers recognise that there is a financial crisis and implement policy actions to deal with it, the crisis would have been full blown and confidence would have been shaken to the point that panic, fear, and pessimism prevail. Expansionary monetary policy does not work to increase output demand as the increase in liquidity does not translate into credit for consumption and investment spending for the reasons discussed earlier and remains mainly as bank reserves. We call this a liquidity trap.[10] Note that even

---

[9] This debt deflation theory is due to Fisher (1933).

[10] In the liquidity trap according to textbook analysis, when nominal interest rates are at 0% expansionary monetary policy is ineffective. Under normal conditions, any excess money balances created by expansionary monetary policy are used to buy bonds, pushing up the price of bonds and lowering the interest rate. However, at 0% nominal interest rate, since bonds earn no interest any excess money balances are merely hoarded by wealth holders. Since nominal interest rates cannot be driven below 0%, any expansion of the money supply does not stimulate investment, rendering monetary policy ineffective. Notice that the liquidity trap according to this analysis relies on the existence of 0% interest rates or extremely low nominal interest rates.

though expansionary monetary policy does not work to increase output demand, it is still necessary to expand liquidity to forestall potential bank failure due to illiquidity. While fiscal policy does work to increase public demand and fill up the output gap created by the fall in private demand, fiscal policy works with a long lag. The lag becomes longer for countries that have no ready plans and designs for public projects that can be brought forward for immediate implementation. Under those circumstances, without ready plans and ready designs, government departments would have to be instructed to put up proposals for projects, have the projects approved and put up detailed designs of the projects before calling for tenders from contractors, and so on.[11] The danger for fiscal policy is that, if a nation does not run prudent fiscal policies in good times and still has to rely on fiscal stimuli in bad times, it is likely to find funding its budget deficits become progressively more expensive and difficult. When budget deficits accumulate to the point that lenders are unwilling to finance them, then the nation would be subject to a fiscal or debt crisis.

CURRENCY OR EXCHANGE-RATE CRISIS

A currency or exchange-rate *crisis* occurs when a sudden loss of international confidence in the value of a nation's currency leads to a rapid fall in the value of its currency and contraction in economic activity.[12] Although a currency crisis usually affects emerging market economies, such as Mexico in 1994; Thailand, Malaysia, Indonesia, and South Korea during the Asian Financial Crisis in 1997–1998; and Argentina in 2001–2002, it can also affect developed nations. Iceland, which has one of the highest per capita incomes in the world,

[11] The lags in fiscal policy due to government departments not having ready projects and therefore not being able to mobilise resources quickly to put fiscal policy into immediate effect was emphasised to me by Professor Lim Chong Yah.

[12] As noted in footnote 5, I do not consider the causes of the crisis. On the causes of currency crises, see Allen *et al.* (2002), who also survey the balance sheet approach to financial crises. This is the approach adopted in this chapter.

not only suffered a banking crisis but also a currency crisis in the wake of the recent US financial crisis and its contagion to the rest of the world.

The main factors determining how adverse an economy subject to a currency crisis will be are maturity mismatch and currency mismatch.[13] As explained earlier, a maturity mismatch occurs when liabilities are short term while assets are long term. A currency mismatch occurs when assets are denominated in domestic currency and liabilities are denominated in foreign currency such that net worth is sensitive to changes in the exchange rate. The implication of the maturity mismatch is that short-term capital inflows are used to finance a current account deficit in the country. Any speculative attack against the country's domestic currency would mean reversing the short-term capital flows and depreciating the currency if the central bank has insufficient foreign reserves to defend the exchange rate. The implication of the currency mismatch is that with foreign-currency denominated debt, depreciating the domestic currency increases the domestic-currency value of liabilities of borrowing firms and banks and decreases their net worth. When the net worth of borrowing firms and banks becomes negative, the firms and banks become insolvent and fail.

To see how currency mismatch can cause bank failure, consider the bank in Table 4 with its balance sheet denominated in domestic-currency units (DCU).

Table 4: Bank balance sheet in DCU.

Assets		Liabilities and net worth	
Reserves	8 DCU	Deposits	80 DCU
Loans	92 DCU	Capital	20 DCU
Total	100 DCU	Total	100 DCU

[13] For a book-length discussion of currency mismatches, see Goldstein and Turner (2004).

Suppose the bank borrows 40 foreign-currency units (FCU) abroad to finance loans denominated in DCU at the exchange rate of 1 FCU = 1 DCU. Then its balance sheet can be shown as Table 5.

With the bank having borrowed heavily abroad in FCU, suppose international currency speculators lose confidence in DCU and sell down DCU to a new value of 1 FCU = 2 DCU. The bank's borrowings of 40 FCU are now worth 80 DCU. Total liabilities equal 80 DCU of borrowings plus 80 DCU of deposits, summing up to 160 DCU. As assets are worth 140 DCU, net worth equals 140 DCU of assets minus 160 DCU of liabilities, i.e., net worth equals –20 DCU. The bank's capital is now negative. The bank has become insolvent, with the balance sheet summarised in Table 6.

If many banks and firms suffer from a currency mismatch, the insolvency of banks will create a banking crisis, which in turn intensifies the currency crisis, creating a vicious cycle of twin crises feeding on each other. The collapse of a currency will also lead to high inflation, high nominal interest rates, and reduced cash flows for firms and households, resulting in a loss of output demand and economic activity. Deteriorating households' and firms' balance sheets and reduced cash flows reduce the ability of households and firms to repay debts, resulting in more bad debts for banks. More

Table 5: Bank balance sheet in DCU and FCU.

Assets		Liabilities and net worth	
Reserves	8 DCU	Deposits	80 DCU
Loans	132 DCU	Borrowings	40 FCU
		Capital	20 DCU

Table 6: Bank balance sheet in DCU and FCU.

Assets		Liabilities and net worth	
Reserves	8 DCU	Deposits	80 DCU
Loans	132 DCU	Borrowings	40 FCU
		Capital	–20 DCU

bank losses lead to more bank failures, more contraction of bank credit, and steep reduction in economic activity. As the currency crisis and banking crisis feed on each other, the economy is trapped in a vicious cycle of contracting economic activity.

What policy options are available to minimise the impact of currency crises? Unfortunately, monetary policy in the presence of capital mobility does not work. If expansionary monetary policy is used, the depreciation of the currency simply amplifies the negative consequences explained earlier. If contractionary monetary policy is used to raise interest rates to induce capital inflows to strengthen the domestic currency, the high interest rates have the effect of contracting output demand and economic activity. A more viable option is to implement capital controls, fix the exchange rate, and then implement an expansionary monetary policy.[14] This was the set of policy options adopted by Malaysia in September 1998 and proved effective in aiding its recovery from the Asian Financial Crisis.

CONCLUDING REMARKS

The destruction of the net worth of banks, firms, and households in a financial crisis is the key factor that has such an adverse impact on the economy. By increasing default risks across both borrowers and lenders, the destruction of net worth worsens adverse selection and moral hazard problems. This means that, in the absence of deposit insurance or in the presence of limited deposit insurance, savers are unwilling to channel their savings into banks. It also means that even if savings are channelled into banks in the presence of full deposit

---

[14] This is an application of what is called the open-economy policy trilemma or unholy trinity in International Macroeconomics. According to the policy trilemma, the three policy goals of exchange-rate stability, free capital mobility, and autonomy in monetary policy cannot co-exist simultaneously. Only two of the three policy goals can be attained at any one time. Since exchange-rate stability and autonomy in monetary policy are incompatible with free capital mobility, capital controls would have to be implemented to attain a fixed exchange rate and independence in monetary policy. The open-economy policy trilemma is due to Mundell (1963) and Fleming (1962).

insurance, banks are still unwilling to extend credit. The resultant drastic cut in credit availability reduces steeply spending on consumption and investment and, hence, output and employment. To the extent that it reduces aggregate spending drastically, a financial crisis is very costly in terms of the loss of output and employment.

Financial crises are crises of bank illiquidity and insolvency. To resolve the bank illiquidity problem, the central bank as lender of last resort can inject massive amounts of liquidity. But expansionary monetary policy is unlikely to work to stimulate private demand because of the liquidity trap created by the rise in default risks and asymmetric information problems. To resolve the bank solvency problem, the government will usually step in to bail out banks that are deemed too big to fail. The costs of insolvency that would otherwise have been borne by bank shareholders and creditors are thus transferred to taxpayers. To the extent that it destroys banks' net worth, a financial crisis can be costly for the government to bail out banks.

While fiscal policy can be employed to increase public demand to replace the loss of private demand, it works with long lags and poses additional problems for governments in that further costs can be incurred down the road as government borrowings add on to public debts and pose potential debt problems, as Portugal, Ireland, Greece, and Spain (PIGS) in the Euro-zone are encountering.

Although policy options are available to fight financial crises, governments and central banks are usually unprepared for them. Whenever financial crises occur, it is usually the case that the economic house is already on fire before the government and central bank send out their economic fire engines. Although ultimately they do douse the economic flame, the damage is already done. The way to handle financial crises is to prevent them. That means regulating the financial system to internalise the external costs that financial institutions, in taking risks and potentially contributing to system-wide failure of the financial system, impose upon the financial system. It also means having the right system of incentives so that private and public interests are better aligned.

REFERENCES

Allen, Mark, Christoph Rosenberg, Christian Keller, Brad Setser and Nouriel Roubini (2002). *A Balance Sheet Approach to Financial Crisis*, IMF Working Paper.

Caprio, Gerard, Daniela Klingebiel, Luc Laeven and Guillermo Noguera (2003). *Banking Crises Database*, World Bank.

Fisher, Irving (1933). The debt-deflation theory of great depressions. *Econometrica*, 1, 337–357.

Fleming, J. Marcus (1962). Domestic financial policies under fixed and under floating exchange rates. *Staff Papers*, International Monetary Fund, 9, 369–379.

Goldstein, Morris and Philip Turner (2004). *Controlling Currency Mismatches in Emerging Markets*. Washington, DC: Peterson Institute.

Gorton, Gary (2010). *Slapped by the Invisible Hand: The Panic of 2007*. New York: Oxford University Press.

Johnson, Simon and James Kwak (2010). *13 Bankers: The Wall Street Takeover and the Next Financial Meltdown*. New York: Pantheon.

Mundell, Robert A. (1963). Capital mobility and stabilization policy under fixed and flexible exchange rates. *Canadian Journal of Economics and Political Science*, 29, 475–485.

Stiglitz, Joseph E. and Andrew Weiss (1981). Credit rationing in markets with imperfect information. *American Economic Review*, 71, 393–410.

Chapter 4

A CASE FOR SELECTIVE CAPITAL CONTROL*

LIM Chong Yah and Sarah CHAN

There are many forms of capital control, many of which are detrimental to the growth of trade, visible and invisible trade, to factor flow and exchange-rate flexibility, and therefore to sustainable growth and development. However, some speculative inflow and outflow of money, especially extreme in scope and volume, can be detrimental to orderly exchange-rate adjustments. An advocacy that such a purely speculative concerted money movement be placed under a selective prevention and intervention list is made out in the interest of overall orderly exchange-rate adjustment as a means for the promotion of more trade, more factor flows, and more sustainable growth and development. Prior preparedness in effective intervention, where and when necessary, is also advocated in the scenario planning of any foreign-exchange jurisdiction.

* Presented at the workshop on *Exchange Rate Systems and Macroeconomic Policies in Asia: Lessons from Past Experiences and Outlooks amid the Global Economic Slowdown* on 11 August 2009 at the Nanyang Executive Centre, NTU.

BALANCE OF PAYMENTS

The balance of payments of a country may be decomposed into seven distinct parts. And each part can have its own capital control. The seven distinct and distinguishable parts are:

Current Account:

(1) balance of visible trade,
(2) balance of invisible trade,
(3) balance of earned transfer,

Capital Account:

(4) balance of foreign direct investment (FDI),
(5) balance of real estate investment,
(6) balance of equity investment, and
(7) balance of unrequited transfer.

Balance of Visible Trade

Item (1), balance of visible trade, is also referred to as balance of merchandise trade. Food, fuel, cars, refrigerators, ships, aircraft, guns and tanks, and other merchandise are grouped together under this item, which normally constitutes the most important part of the balance of payments. If capital control is used for this item or any part of it, it in fact amounts to trade control. Capital control is just used as a means for trade control. However, trade control can also be used as a means for capital control.

Balance of Invisible Trade

With globalisation, the ease of transport and communication, and the mounting and endless movement of people, invisible trade has become increasingly a very important component of total trade. Invisible trade includes tourism, shipping, civil aviation, telecommunication, banking, and insurance services. Item (2), balance of invisible trade, plus item (1), balance of visible trade, make up the balance of trade. Much of the discussion and disputes in international trade conferences cover this composite item, the trade item, particularly by the visible trade subset.

Current Account Balance

Foreign workers' remittances and income from foreign investments fall under earned transfer item (3). The balance of trade and the balance of transfer constitute the balance of current account. This current account balance is often used, and wrongly used, for negotiations on foreign-exchange adjustments, and worst still, on a bilateral basis, whereas trade and transfers are done on a global and multi-lateral basis. Overall balance on current account, however, may be used as an indication of export competitiveness or otherwise. An overall persistent fundamental deficit on current account is a signal of export non-competitiveness of the economy. This is not quite the same as the balance with any trading partner. An oil importing country such as Japan can have a trade deficit with an oil exporting country, such as Saudi Arabia, and yet she may have an overall balance on current account with other countries to make up for an overall surplus. Thus, trade balance and current account balance cannot be viewed with one commodity only or with one country only. Trade negotiations done on the basis of one commodity or one country on a *quid pro quo* basis is detrimental to the multi-lateral trading system, especially if the rate of exchange is also reviewed on that basis. The rate of exchange is multi-laterally determined.

When we advocate capital control, we do not mean the use of capital control to limit trade flow or current account flow. For items (1), (2), and (3), merchandise trade, invisible trade, and earned transfer, it is definitely detrimental to have capital control, which should be and must be avoided. Similar avoidance must be made to negotiate for exchange-rate adjustment based on a commodity or a group of select commodities or based on two countries or a group of select countries. The overall picture, the overall balance, should be looked at, for it is the overall balance that determines the exchange rate.

Capital account items (4), (5), (6), and (7) are shown separately from current account items (1), (2), and (3). The former deals with capital flows for direct investment commonly known as FDIs, property investment, equity investment, and cash balance transfers. Equity investment is also referred to as portfolio investment. A line should be drawn between the transaction motive of such capital flows and the speculative motive. The distinction lies in the weightage of the speculative motive. All investments have some "speculative" component in the sense of looking into the future. A speculative motive plus the transaction cost component can be used to jointly decide on the division of whether there should be capital control. FDIs have high transaction costs. One cannot pull in and pull out FDIs that easily without incurring high costs. The same can be said of property investment. In the interest of encouraging capital flow and the flow of enterprise, in our view, there should be no capital restriction on such items — items (4) and (5), foreign direct investment and foreign real estate investment.

CAPITAL CONTROL ITEMS

Of the seven items, we have advocated no capital control whatsoever for items (1) to (5): visible trade, invisible trade, earned transfer, foreign direct investment, and real estate investment. We are now left with only two items, (6) and (7). These last two items — equity investment (6) and unrequited transfer (7) share a common feature, and that is, the ease with which such investment may be transferred in and out of the country. Highly speculative capital inflow and outflow can create havoc to the exchange-rate system through these two sources, particularly item (7), unrequited transfer.

To ameliorate the sudden and massive outflow of funds resulting in a bottomless fall in the exchange rate, as in the 1997/98 exchange-rate crisis in both Thailand and Indonesia, the regulators may wish to consider some restrictions to the complete free flow of capital (money) for these two items. These restrictions may include (a) the giving of at least a week's notice after receiving the proceed from the sale of the equities in the bank balance before external transfer and (b) the amount does not exceed, say, US$10 million for an individual and $100 million for institutions for any single transaction in a day, unless prior permission of the regulator has been obtained. Note that if the cash balance is kept within the country, such barriers of transfer do not apply. They do not create an exchange-rate crisis. Thus, under our advocacy there is maximum freedom or no restriction in buying and selling of items (1) to (5). Minimal preventive restriction is only for items (6) and (7) and only applicable to big ticket unrequited transfers. Of course, in a serious exchange-rate crisis, the regulators should look into further temporary barriers. These barriers against speculative exchange outflow are much easier to manage in a managed float regime than in a fixed rate regime or a completely free-float regime. Most countries are in the managed float system at any rate. The managed float system is no longer ridiculed by the US and the International Monetary Fund (IMF) as "dirty float", as in the past.

CAPITAL CONTROL PREPAREDNESS

The preparedness of regulators in terms of already enacted legislation and prior agreed regulatory procedures is also important, if last minute panic and built-in uncontrollable porousness are to be avoided. In other words, the administrative infrastructure and the legality of the preventive regulations have to be there first and to be utilised only if needed. As an aside, I recall my conversation with Dr Soedradjad Djiwandono, the former Governor of the Central Bank of Indonesia. When asked why Indonesia did not introduce capital control as Malaysia did during the exchange crisis of 1997/98, he replied that there had been no prior preparedness for capital control. Thus, in his excellent book on the crisis in Indonesia (Djiwandono, 2005), there was no mention of capital control at all. Indonesia then was under IMF tutelage, and the IMF was very transparent in not considering capital control, any form, as a viable option. The IMF firmly believed in exchange-rate *laissez-faireism* and for any country, big or small, and under whatever fiscal and balance-of-payment circumstances. Capital control ran counter to the doctrine of the so-called Washington Consensus under which the IMF operated, and is still operating, though the term Washington Consensus has dropped out of popular and IMF usage.

It bears repetition to state that capital control can take many forms but the capital control we have in mind relates only to the prevention and aggravation of an exchange-rate crisis. The control is minimal and is operational in a managed float or free-floating regime and affects only big ticket exchange-rate speculators.

TWO MONEY VALUES

Money has two values: the internal value and the external value. There are many kinds of rules and regulations to ensure that the internal value is stable. Why not the external value? When one has a freely floating exchange-rate system, it means that the exchange-rate is not stable; it fluctuates freely according to the demand for and supply of that currency. Should not there be some rules and regulations to promote the short-term stability of the exchange rate? Indeed, in a managed float system, such short-term stability is aimed at through the deliberate buying and selling of foreign-exchange reserves. Long-term necessary exchange-rate adjustments can be taken care of by the managed float process. A *laissez-faire* exchange-rate mechanism is not as self-adjusting as it should be in theory, besides the uncontrolled and uncontrollable damage it can make to visible trade, invisible trade, FDI flow, and the economy as a whole.

INTERNATIONAL GOLD STANDARD

Before 1972 when the US dollar was pegged to gold at a fixed rate of US$35 to one fine ounce of gold, in an important sense, the US dollar was stable, stable against gold. It meant there must be enough gold at Fort Knox to exchange for US dollars at that fixed rate. Once there was not enough gold left at Fort Knox, speculators would make a run on Fort Knox, and the USA was consequently forced to go off the international gold standard. The USA thus opted for a free-floating regime since then, and others, a variety of responses including the present more ubiquitous managed float systems.

GOLD EXCHANGE STANDARD

When the US dollar was fixed to gold and had free convertibility with gold, the other currencies that were all fixed to the US dollar then were also stable. Changes to parity must be with the agreement of the IMF. The system ushered in a period of unprecedented prosperity, including in the USA. After that crisis in 1971, when US went off gold, the global affluence continued unabated, with most countries, as stated earlier, adopting a managed float exchange-rate system. Managed floating brings in exchange stability with flexibility, just like under the previous international gold standard system. The US dollar continued to serve as a pivotal currency, as a reserve currency, and as a prime international medium of exchange.

THE THREE CRISES

Since 1971, however, the global monetary system seriously failed thrice. One was in 1973/74, which resulted in global stagflation. The next one was in 1997/98 affecting mainly some superlative growth rate countries in Asia. The third is the present sub-prime originated economic crisis. The first and the third originated from the USA, and both could be attributed to an oversupply of US credit money. A separate paper on the present crisis termed by the writer as the Great Recession has been presented at the Singapore Economic Review Conference a few days ago (Lim, 2009a).

CAPITAL CONTROL AND GDP GROWTH

The second crisis in 1997/98 can be easily traced to the fundamental disequilibrium problem of Asian countries such as Thailand, Malaysia, and Indonesia, together with its contagious and serious "tom-yam effect" on others such as Singapore and Hong Kong. Those

Table 1: Changes in real per capita income of capital control and non-capital control ASEAN countries 1996 and 2004 (US$).

Countries	% Increase
Capital control	
Cambodia	+9.0
Laos	+56.3
Myanmar	+17.7
Vietnam	+66.0
Non-capital control	
Brunei	−16.7
Indonesia	−10.4
Malaysia	−2.0
Philippines	−10.7
Singapore	−2.6
Thailand	−18.3

Source: Lim, 2007, p. 286.

conspicuously spared from the "tom-yam effect" were Asian countries that had capital control in one form or another, such as China, Vietnam, and India. Even when the recovery process later came in, it was the Southeast Asian countries that originally had capital control recovered the fastest, as can be seen from the Table 1.

CHINA, INDIA, AND VIETNAM

Other findings also support the effectiveness of capital controls in promoting or restoring economic stability. Kaplan and Rodrik (2001), for instance, appraised the relative performance of the Malaysian crisis resolution measures with focus on capital controls of 1998 in relation to those IMF-sponsored orthodox packages adopted in Korea and Thailand. Through the use of a "time-shifted differences-in-difference technique" for building appropriate counterfactuals, they concluded that the controls were effective by allowing a faster recovery than otherwise.

Using daily financial data, Edison and Reinhart (2001) concluded that capital controls imposed by Malaysia in 1998 had helped the country achieve greater interest rate and exchange rate stability and more policy autonomy. Indeed, the imposition of capital controls was often deemed necessary for countries afflicted by financial crisis. An unpublished doctoral dissertation which examined the causal linkage between capital account liberalisation and currency crisis in four countries — Thailand, Malaysia, Korea, and Chile — found that a reduction in portfolio capital outflows have led to smaller currency crisis indexes, indicating that capital control measures were found to have reduced the risks of currency instability faced by these countries (Hu, 2003).

It is not true that countries that had capital control would be adversely affected in growth and development. China, Vietnam, and India are examples of high-growth countries that had and still have capital control. According to an unpublished NTU doctoral dissertation (Dong, 2004), it is dangerous for China to liberalise its capital account prematurely, given the weakness of its domestic banking system. Without capital controls, China's economic growth could lose its momentum. There will be a danger of capital fleeing the country, resulting in insufficient investment to sustain economic growth.

The experiences of China and also India seem to suggest that the long-standing and extensive controls on capital transactions may have had some role to play in reducing the vulnerability of these countries to financial crisis (IMF, 2000). In particular, they helped shift the composition of capital inflows towards long-term flows, which is critical for economic growth. For other East Asian countries, historically both Japan and Taiwan grew very rapidly in the 1950s, 1960s, 1970s, and 1980s, capital control notwithstanding.

USA AND CAPITAL CONTROL

This presentation, however, is not to propose a case for capital control for the USA, being the supplier of the global anchor currency, the US dollar. Since the US dollar has been and is the main means of international exchange and also serves as a store of value function internationally, the whole monetary structure would change if the USA starts having exchange control. All the USA needs to do is to avoid having a runaway balance-of-payments deficit, i.e. a persistent runaway balance-of-payments deficit through too big a fiduciary issue. But if the USA continues to have the Dutch disease and if the Dutch disease continues to be uncontrollable, resulting in uncontrollable US exchange-rate depreciation, a case for capital control even for the USA should not be completely ruled out, especially if that uncontrollable depreciation could result in global competitive devaluation.

If a country other than the USA has some forms of precautionary exchange control, strictly nominal or otherwise, it does not follow that they should not have more exchange control in times of unexpected balance-of-payment crisis, as had come to pass in Malaysia in 1998. It was the introduction and implementation of capital control in Malaysia in 1998 that saved the Malaysian economy from collapsing, as had happened to neighbouring Thailand and Indonesia that came under the direction of IMF, which opted not to have capital control and had, *inter alia*, runs on the banks instead (Lim, 2009b). Indonesia, in fact, even lost the Government that invited IMF for aid, reminiscent of Macbeth killing Duncan to solve the former's problem.

FINANCIAL CENTRES

It may be argued that some jurisdictions like Hong Kong and Singapore will eschew capital control, as they are financial centres. Control is inimical to the growth of such centres. However, some discreet intervention may work for orderliness and prevent excessive gyrations in exchange rates. Besides, prevention and intervention can have a curative or remedial function, which will contribute to the stability of a financial centre. Of course control has to be very minimal, nominal in normal times and non-applicable to most investors, domestic or foreign. And at all times, control of (1) to (5) should be avoided. Selective control should be confined only to (6) and (7) when and if necessary, either as a preventive measure or as an interventional one. Financial life must go on, and must be seen to go on, uninterrupted, unhampered, and unchained. The financial policeman, however, should be there and should be depended on for timely help, if and when necessary. A completely unregulated market is a messy one, like the fallen leaves in a jungle, even for financial centres. Discreet and prudential regulations are meant to promote growth, not to stifle it. The market is made for man and not man for the market.

That Singapore has a managed float system and Hong Kong a Currency Board System, implying a fixed rate of exchange vis-à-vis the US dollar, are signs of measures, each in its own way, for an orderly exchange-rate regime. In the case of Hong Kong, the emphasis is on internal macroeconomic flexibility and adjustment, although in practice, Singapore appears to advocate and practice, and has more room to practice, more internal flexibility, and adjustment than Hong Kong. But the Hong Kong's exchange-rate system is perfectly workable, if there is no serious pressure on upward adjustment by a persistent rising US dollar. This, a persistent rising US dollar trend, is most unlikely to happen in the foreseeable future. Indeed, the opposite is more likely to happen, and thus the system does not constitute an Achilles' heel for Hong Kong in the current and foreseeable circumstances.

RESERVES AND SWAPS

Besides, the exchange-rate system can be cushioned and strengthened by the stockpile of surplus foreign-exchange reserves, supplemented by exchange swap arrangements on a bilateral and multi-lateral basis, as is taking place in many countries in East Asia. But this international mutual help arrangement in a crisis is perfectly consistent with domestic selective capital control as a second or third line of defence. Similarly, this international mutual help arrangement is consistent with countries seeking IMF help as a last line of defence.

FINAL JUDGEMENT

Our conclusion is that with the existence of nominal and minimal selective capital control arrangement, and with built-in insurance and pre-prepared remedial measures, the exchange-rate regime is less likely to disintegrate and can pass many a stress test. It will be much more promotional to trade, visible and invisible trade, and to short-, medium-, and long-term capital movements and transfers, can thus contribute to much better rates of economic advance and much higher levels of sustainable economic security.

REFERENCES

Djiwandono, J. Soedradjad (2005). *Bank Indonesia and the Crisis: An Insider's View.* Singapore: ISEAS.

Dong, Zhiyong (2004). *China's Capital Account Liberalization: Issues and Options,* Unpublished PhD dissertation, Nanyang Technological University.

Edison, H. and C. M. Reinhart (2001). Stopping hot money. *Journal of Development Economics,* 66(2), 533–553.

Hu, Chia-Chih (2003). *Capital Account Liberalization and Currency Crisis: Cases of Thailand, Korea, Malaysia and Chile.* Unpublished PhD dissertation, Nanyang Business School, Nanyang Technological University.

Kaplan, E. and D. Rodrik (2001). Did the Malaysian capital controls work? NBER Chapters. In *Preventing Currency Crises in Emerging Markets,* pp. 393–440. National Bureau of Economic Research, Inc.

Lim, Chong Yah (2006). How the IMF can stay relevant, *The Straits Times,* 7 September 2006.

Lim, Chong Yah (2009a). *Unpreparedness in the Great Recession.* Special Lecture given at the opening of the Singapore Economic Review Conference (SERC) 2009 on 6 August 2009 at the Swissotel, Singapore.

Lim, Chong Yah (2009b). The Asian Financial Crisis. In *Southeast Asia: The Long Road Ahead,* (3rd Ed.) Singapore: World Scientific.

Part 2

Public Policies and Other Economic Issues

Chapter 5

COMPETITION POLICY AND LAW IN SINGAPORE

LAM Chuan Leong*

The start of generic competition law in Singapore can be traced back to 2003 when the Economic Review Committee recommended that a law to create a level playing field for businesses be enacted. Under the new law, businesses would be able to operate under more conducive business conditions and compete on an equal footing. The government accepted the recommendation and generic competition law was enacted in 2004. Subsequently, the Competition Commission of Singapore (CCS), a statutory board under the purview of the Ministry of Trade and Industry, was established in 2005 to administer and enforce the Competition Act. This chapter seeks to trace the trajectory of the development of Competition Law in Singapore and provide an overview of the main features of the Competition Act, as well as some insights on the regulatory philosophy and policy thinking principles of the CCS.

INTRODUCTION

The start of modern Competition Policy and Law can be traced back to the late 19th century when the United States passed the Sherman

* I am grateful to Ms Yvette Yoong (Assistant Director) and Mr Harikumar SP (Assistant Director) for their assistance in the preparation of this chapter.

Act of 1890 and the Clayton Act of 1914. The growth of Competition Policy in Europe began in 1957 when Belgium, France, Italy, Luxembourg, the Netherlands, and West Germany signed the Treaty of the European Community (EC Treaty or Treaty of Rome 1957), which over the last 50 years has grown into what is now the European Union made up of 27 member countries and nearly half a billion citizens.

Closer to home, countries in the ASEAN region have been becoming more exposed to Competition Policy and Law. ASEAN leaders have confirmed their commitment to the development of a more integrated, dynamic, and vibrant regional economy by accelerating the timetable for realisation of the ASEAN Economic Community to 2015.[1] The ASEAN Economic Community Blueprint of 20 November 2007 provides for the development of a regional guideline on Competition Policy by 2010, based on country experiences and international best practices with the view to creating a fair competition environment. As committed under the Blueprint, ASEAN Member States shall endeavour to introduce Competition Policy by 2015. Interaction in the region between ASEAN Member States is effected through the ASEAN Experts Group on Competition ("AEGC"), which focuses on capacity building for the implementation of Competition Policy and Law, and on developing the above mentioned regional guidelines, as a first step for a more coordinated approach to Competition Policy and Law within the ASEAN region. To this end, the AEGC is developing Regional Guidelines on Competition Policy, which will serve as a general framework guide for the ASEAN Member States as they endeavour to introduce, implement, and develop national Competition Policy and Law. In addition to the capacity building initiatives, to date, Indonesia, Thailand, and Vietnam[2] have also implemented

[1] Information Pack on ASEAN-EU Program for Regional Integration Support — APRIS Phase II.

[2] Both the adoption and implementation of Competition Law and Policy in Indonesia and Thailand began in 1999. The Law on Competition was approved by Vietnam's National Assembly at its November 2004 Session and came into force on 1 July 2005.

Competition frameworks into their markets and continue to share experiences with its neighbours in order to ensure smooth implementation of their competition regimes. Malaysia is next in line and the country is looking to pass its Competition Bill in 2010.

COMPETITION LAW IN SINGAPORE

In 2003, the Economic Review Committee chaired by the then Deputy Prime Minister Lee Hsien Loong recommended the enactment of a generic Competition Law to create a pro-enterprise environment in Singapore.[3] In the second reading speech for the Competition Bill, the then Senior Minister of State for Trade and Industry, Dr Vivian Balakrishnan said:

> "Competition is a key tenet of Singapore's economic strategy. Market competition spurs firms to be more efficient, innovative, and responsive to consumer needs. Consumers would enjoy more choices, lower prices, and better products and services. The economy as a whole benefits from greater productivity gains and more efficient resource allocation. Therefore, wherever appropriate, Singapore has opened up sectors of the economy to market competition."

The introduction of generic Competition Law was timely for two reasons.[4] First, a pro-competitive environment would serve to reinforce Singapore's efforts to foster enterprise development and nurture start-ups. Second, Competition Law will further enhance the efficiency of the country's markets and strengthen our economic competitiveness in the face of intensifying international competition.

The Competition Act in Singapore was passed by the Parliament in late 2004 after about 6 months of active consultation on the draft

---

[3] See page 60 of Ong Beng Lee, "*Promoting Competition: The CCS Perspective*", Regulation and the Limits of Competition, Economics Symposium Series — Centre for Governance and Leadership — Civil Service College, in collaboration with Institute of Policy Studies and Economic Society of Singapore.

[4] *Ibid.*

Bill. The Act is largely modelled on the UK's Competition Act 1998. A transitional period of more than a year was provided before prohibitions against anti-competitive agreements and abuse of a dominant position came into effect on 1 January 2006. Although the Act only came into force in 2006, competition has and continues to be a key tenet of Singapore's economic strategy. As a result of its open trade and investment policies, businesses in Singapore have always been subjected to global competition for decades and are continually striving to strengthen their competitiveness.[5]

The Competition Commission of Singapore, CCS, a statutory board under the Ministry of Trade and Industry, was established on 1 January 2005, to administer and enforce Competition Law in Singapore. CCS aims to promote healthy competitive markets that will benefit the Singapore economy, based on sound economic principles applied objectively and consistently. CCS does not deal with consumer protection, although the competition authorities in some jurisdictions, such as UK and Australia, have this consumer protection role.

The importance of competition in Singapore's economic growth was underscored by the President of Singapore in his address at the opening of Parliament on 18 May 2009:

> "Our basic approach to promoting growth has been to stay competitive, upgrade our people, develop new capabilities, and create an outstanding pro-business environment. Then we can rely on free markets, free trade and entrepreneurship to create wealth for individuals and the country. This is how Singapore has consistently developed year after year, and over time totally transformed our economy and our people's lives."

The Competition Act provides only for civil financial penalties to be imposed on an offending business that infringes the Act. Unlike in the UK or in the US, we do not have criminal penalties

---

[5] See Toh Han Li, *Enforcement Against Cartels Under Singapore Law*, at page 2, paragraph 3.

against the businesses or individuals concerned. The third and final prohibition under the Act, which is against mergers that will substantially lessen competition, came into effect on 1 July 2007.

Scope of the Act

The Act applies to all undertakings capable of commercial and economic activity, regardless of whether they are foreign-owned or Singapore-owned. In addition to the above, companies owned by the Singapore Government and statutory boards also come under the purview of the Act.

However, the Act does not apply to activities, agreements, and conduct of the Government, statutory bodies or entities acting on their behalf. This is because the intent of Competition Law is to regulate the conduct of market players, and not the Government and statutory boards that perform public functions. Notwithstanding this, CCS has been conducting outreach and advocacy activities amongst other Government agencies in order to raise public-sector awareness of the Competition Act and to encourage compliance with the Act. In addition, certain activities and sectors of the economy, such as those which come under the purview of sector-specific regulators, are excluded from the Competition Act.[6]

In order to balance regulatory and business compliance costs against the benefits that can be accrued from effective competition, the principal focus of the Competition Act will be on those anti-competitive activities that have an appreciable adverse effect on competition or those that do not have any net economic benefit (NEB). In this regard, CCS also accords due weight to whether an activity or conduct promotes innovation, brings about economic efficiency in the longer term, or results in increased

---

[6] See page 61 of Ong Beng Lee, *Promoting Competition: The CCS Perspective*, Regulation and the Limits of Competition, Economics Symposium Series — Centre for Governance and Leadership — Civil Service College, in collaboration with the Institute of Policy Studies and Economic Society of Singapore.

productivity — mindful that the law and policy should not constrain innovation and entrepreneurship.[7]

MAIN FEATURES OF SINGAPORE'S COMPETITION ACT

Anti-Competitive Agreements

Section 34 of the Act prohibits agreements between undertakings, decisions by associations of undertakings or concerted practices which have as their object or effect the prevention of, restriction, or distortion of competition within Singapore. The term "agreements" has a wide meaning; agreements can fall within the scope of Section 34 whether they are legally enforceable or non-enforceable, whether they are written or oral. Section 34 also covers concerted practices, where even though there is no formal agreement or decision taken, there is deemed to be informal co-operation between the parties. The prohibition applies even if the agreement was entered into outside Singapore or if the party to the agreement is outside Singapore.

CCS, has, in its Guidelines, identified four main types of cartel conduct (price fixing, bid rigging, market-sharing, and output limitations[8]) as always having an appreciable adverse effect on competition[9] by their very nature. An example of an agreement that is likely to infringe the Section 34 prohibition is price-fixing. There are many ways in which firms can price-fix. Such agreements can involve reaching a consensus on the prices to be charged or establishing a range

[7] Cavinder Bull, Lim Chong Kin, and Richard Whish, *Competition Law and Policy in Singapore* (Academy Publishing, 2009), at pages 10–11.

[8] See paragraphs 3.3–3.12 of the *CCS Guidelines on the Section 34 Prohibition* for elaboration of such conduct. Examples of other agreements that may infringe the Section 34 prohibition are set out at paragraphs 3.13–3.29.

[9] See paragraph 2.20 of the *CCS Guidelines on the Section 34 Prohibition*. This is notwithstanding that the market shares of the parties are below the threshold levels mentioned in paragraph 2.19 of the same, and even if the parties to such agreements are SMEs. Nonetheless, market share of the parties is one of the factors that CCS will consider when determining the appropriate penalties to be imposed on the parties; see paragraph 2.3 of the *CCS Guidelines on the Appropriate Amount of Penalty*.

outside which prices are not to move. They may also take the form of an agreement not to quote prices without consulting potential competitors, or to not charge below any other price in the market.

Object or effect

Section 34 of the Act states that:

> "**34.**—(1) Subject to Section 35, agreements between undertakings, decisions by associations of undertakings or concerted practices which have as their *object or effect* the prevention, restriction or distortion of competition within Singapore are prohibited unless they are exempt in accordance with the provisions of this Part." [emphasis added]

Whether agreements have as its object or effect the prevention, restriction, or distortion of competition is central in the analysis of a case under Section 34 of the Act. Given that the prohibition in Section 34 of the Act is against decisions which have as their "object or effect" the prevention, restriction, or distortion of competition, this must be read ***disjunctively***. Hence, once it is established that a decision has as its "object" the prevention, restriction, or distortion of competition, it is unnecessary to further prove that the agreement/decision has any "effects" in order to find an infringement.[10]

The idea is that some agreements are so obviously, restrictive of competition and so, unlikely to have any redeeming features, that precious resources should not be wasted to prove the breach, to establish the anti-competitive effect of the agreement. Where it is shown that the object of the agreement is to restrict competition, the onus will be on the parties to the agreement to defend it and to establish that it meets the NEB criteria.

---

[10] *Société Technique Miniere* [1966] ECR 235; Cases 56 and 58/64 *Consten and Grundig v Commission*, [1966] ECR 299; Case 45/85 *VdS v Commission* [1987] ECR 405.

Effects of an agreement

Where it is not plain that the object of the co-operation is to restrict competition, an analysis of its effects becomes crucial, before it can be determined whether the agreement restricts competition within the meaning of the Section 34 prohibition. The "effects" test requires an examination of the economic conditions prevailing on the market(s) concerned and of the effects of the agreement/ decision on competition.

Some policy issues

(i) Price guidelines
   (a) As a general observation, price recommendations are regarded by competition agencies in most countries as harmful to competition because they may lead to price fixing or clustering of prices around the recommended levels.[11] They also tend to restrict independent pricing decisions;
   (b) Rather than relying on a price issued by the association, it is better for the customer to find out about different rates before deciding on the best deal for himself[12];
   (c) In general, publication of historical information on ranges of prices charged will not constitute anti-competitive practice. On the contrary, it adds to price transparency and informs the consumer choice.

(ii) Price parallelism vs. price fixing
In general, parallel pricing alone would be insufficient to sustain a finding of infringement. An observation that movements of prices are similar across competing companies will

[11] CCS press release, 18 October 2008, Guideline on medical fees: Apply to CCS for guidance.

[12] CCS press release, 1 August 08, CCS advises SSTA to take remedial action on its recommendation of a fuel surcharge.

not, in and of itself, amount to evidence of collusion in these markets, where there is a high degree of market transparency.

(iii) Net economic benefit
An agreement that falls within the scope of Section 34 may, on balance, have an NEB if it contributes to improving production or distribution; or promoting technical or economic progress and it does not impose on the undertakings concerned restrictions, which are not indispensable to the attainment of those objectives or afford the undertakings concerned the possibility of eliminating competition in respect of a substantial part of the goods or services in question. Individual agreements possessing these characteristics are excluded under the Third Schedule.[13]

Abuse of a Dominant Position

The second main prohibition under the Act relates to the abuse of a dominant position. Section 47 of the Act, which came into force on 1 January 2006, prohibits any conduct on the part of one or more undertakings, which is an abuse of a dominant position, in any market in Singapore.[14] The Section 47 prohibition only prohibits abuse of a dominant position. It does not prohibit undertakings from having a dominant position or striving to achieve it. The Section 47 prohibition also applies to undertakings in a dominant position outside Singapore, and which abuse that dominant position in a market in Singapore.[15]

In considering whether there has been an abuse of dominance, CCS will conduct a detailed examination of the relevant markets concerned and the effects of the undertaking's conduct. Specifically, Section 47 prohibits predatory behaviour towards competitors; limiting production, markets, or technical development to the

---

[13] *CCS Guidelines on the Section 34 Prohibition*, paragraph 2.24.

[14] See paragraph 1.1, *CCS Guidelines on the Section 47 Prohibition.*

[15] See paragraphs 2.1 and 2.2, *CCS Guidelines on the Section 47 Prohibition.*

prejudice of consumers; applying dissimilar conditions to equivalent transactions with other trading parties, thereby placing them at a competitive disadvantage; or making the conclusion of contracts subject to acceptance by the other parties of supplementary obligations which, by their nature or according to commercial usage, have no connection with the subject of the contracts.[16]

Generally, as a starting point, CCS will consider a market share of above 60% as likely to indicate that an undertaking is dominant in the relevant market. Similarly, dominance could potentially be established at a lower market share, if other relevant factors provided CCS with strong evidence of dominance.[17] The Section 47 prohibition also includes conduct on the part of two or more undertakings, where there is an abuse of a collective dominant position.[18]

Exclusions to both the Section 34 and the Section 47 prohibitions[19] extend to undertakings entrusted with the operation of services of general economic interest or having character of a revenue-producing monopoly, insofar as the prohibition would obstruct the performance, in law or fact, of the particular tasks assigned to that undertaking. This exclusion is almost identical to that in the EU's competition regime.

CCS not a price regulator

CCS operates as an enforcement agency as opposed to a regulatory body. It is particularly not a price regulator. Section 47 of the Act is modelled closely after Section 18 of the UK Competition Act and after Article 102 of the EC Treaty. However, conspicuously omitted from Section 47 of the Act is the first example of an abuse as set out

---

[16] Refer to Section 47(2) of the Act.

[17] See paragraph 3.8, *CCS Guidelines on the Section 47 Prohibition.*

[18] See paragraph 3.16, *CCS Guidelines on the Section 47 Prohibition.*

[19] Refer to paragraph 5.1, *CCS Guidelines on the Section 47 Prohibition* and Third Schedule of the Act.

in Section 18 of the UK Competition Act and Article 102 of the EC Treaty:

> "...directly or indirectly imposing unfair purchase or selling prices."

Case law in the UK and the EC has deemed this example of an abuse as one that covers both excessively high and low prices, in the case of predatory pricing. Richard Whish points out that the excessively high prices are objected to because they can result in an exploitation of customers by a dominant firm.[20] Furthermore, excessively high prices are objectionable because they effectively amount to a refusal to supply,[21] an alleged form of anti-competitive conduct.

Instead, Section 47 of the Act sets out "*predatory behaviour towards competitors*" as the first example of abusive conduct. This departure from the position taken in both the UK and the EU can be construed as one where the Singapore position focuses clearly on competitive, rather than high prices.

However, this does not rule out the possibility or prevent CCS from making a finding that a firm in a dominant position has, in fact, abused that position by imposing excessively high prices on consumers, especially if it translates into a situation tantamount to that of a refusal to supply.

Mergers that substantially lessen competition

The third main prohibition of the Competition Act relates to mergers that substantially lessen competition or anti-competitive mergers. To that end, Section 54 of the Competition Act prohibits mergers that have resulted, or may be expected to result, in a substantial lessening of competition within any market in Singapore

---

[20] Richard Whish, *Competition Law* (Oxford University Press, 6th Ed., 2008) at pages 709–718.

[21] *Ibid.* at pages 714–718.

for goods or services, unless they are excluded or exempted. In general, a substantial lessening of competition is likely to result in higher prices, lower quality, and/or less choices of products and services for consumers. Within the meaning of the Act, the term "mergers" is interpreted broadly to include not only amalgamations or schemes of arrangement, but may also include acquisitions of undertakings, or the acquisitions of the assets of undertakings.

The Section 54 prohibition came into effect on 1 July 2007. In assessing if the merger results, or is likely to result, in a substantial lessening of competition, CCS will generally consider the ability of the merged firm to profitably raise prices, and the ability of firms in the relevant market to co-ordinate prices following the merger. Merger notifications are applications by merger parties to CCS for a decision as to whether the merger has infringed or whether the anticipated merger if carried into effect will infringe the Section 54 prohibition.

Similar to agreements with NEB, there is an exclusion for mergers that produce net economic efficiencies, which means that mergers which give rise to efficiencies, such as lower costs or higher-quality products, which offset any harm resulting from the loss of competition are excluded from the Section 54 prohibition.

REGULATORY PHILOSOPHY[22]

Unlike the sector-specific regulators which regulate the conduct of market players *ex ante* through licensing conditions etc., generic Competition Law adopts an *ex post* approach. This means that CCS will wait until there are reasonable grounds for suspecting an infringement before taking action. CCS' regulatory philosophy may be summarised according to the following principles.

---

[22] See pages 63–68 of Ong Beng Lee, *Promoting Competition: the CCS Perspective*, Regulation and the Limits of Competition, Economics Symposium Series — Centre for Governance and Leadership — Civil Service College, in collaboration with Institute of Policy Studies and Economic Society of Singapore.

Focus on Anti-Competitive Behaviour with Appreciable Adverse Effect

In enforcing the Competition Act, CCS is mindful of regulatory and business compliance costs, and its own resource constraints. As such, instead of attempting to catch all forms of anti-competitive activities, CCS' focus is on activities that have an appreciable adverse effect on competition in Singapore. Competition is not pursued simply for its own sake — sometimes less competition may result in other benefits such as improvements in research and development. Former Senior Minister of State for Trade and Industry, Dr Vivian Balakrishnan, said during the Second Reading of the Competition Bill that,

> "instead of attempting to catch all forms of anti-competitive activities, our principal focus will be on those that have an appreciable adverse effect on competition in Singapore that do not have any net economic benefit."

Due Consideration Given to Whether Anti-Competitive Activity Generates NEB

In assessing whether an anti-competitive agreement infringes the Competition Act, CCS will take into account whether it promotes innovation, productivity, or longer-term economic efficiency. If these benefits outweigh the likely anti-competitive harm (i.e., there is a NEB to Singapore), CCS will assess that the agreement does not infringe the Act. This approach allows CCS to take into account all relevant considerations before making a determination on a case.

Emphasis on Self-Assessment

In line with its risk-management approach towards possible infringements of the Competition Act, CCS emphasises self-assessment and voluntary compliance by businesses.

CCS has so far published 13 sets of guidelines to help businesses understand how CCS will interpret and give effect to the

Act, so that they can conduct their own self-assessment. This is particularly important, as Competition Law is rather new in Singapore. These guidelines cover the major aspects of CCS' work, such as the existing key prohibitions, market definition, and enforcement. CCS has also issued two sets of guidelines on merger procedures and substantive assessment to help businesses assess whether their mergers are likely to raise competition concerns.

In addition to the published guidelines, CCS' website aims to provide a one-stop access to information on the Competition Act and includes FAQs, forms, and other public documents published by CCS. There is also information to help businesses that are interested in implementing compliance programs get started. Indeed, some businesses have obtained their own legal advice and have put in place such programs.

As Competition Law is rather new in Singapore, CCS has also installed a formal, voluntary notification mechanism to help businesses that want more certainty on whether their conduct or agreement infringes, or is likely to infringe, the Competition Act. They can choose to notify their conduct or agreement for guidance or decision, depending on their need for confidentiality. Notifications for decision provide greater certainty, but public consultation is required, so that CCS can hear out other relevant parties. Businesses are encouraged to undergo self-assessment before formally notifying their agreements or conduct to CCS.

Balancing Advocacy with Strict Enforcement

One of CCS' priorities is to conduct outreach activities and advocate compliance with the Competition Act. CCS has conducted numerous talks and industry briefings, as part of its efforts to increase public awareness, understanding, and support for the Act. CCS continues to balance its advocacy efforts with vigorous enforcement of the Competition Act. It also has the requisite investigative and enforcement powers to do so and is able to impose stiff penalties to serve as deterrence. So far, CCS has exercised its powers to require the production of relevant documents and has also conducted inspections by entering business premises to require the production of relevant documents as well as executed search warrants on business premises.

CCS also has a Leniency Program to encourage businesses that are currently involved in cartel activities to come clean in return for immunity or a reduction in financial penalty. To break up cartels, which are by their nature secretive, informants are critical. The experience in overseas jurisdictions has demonstrated the effectiveness of leniency programs in detecting and breaking up cartels.

Coupled with the Leniency Program, CCS has in place a Leniency Plus program. Under the Leniency Plus program, an undertaking may benefit from a reduction of up to 100% in the financial penalty to be imposed if it came forward with information on a second cartel during CCS' investigations against the said undertaking for its involvement in a separate cartel.

CCS also plays a proactive role in undertaking market inquiries in sectors where it has reasonable grounds for suspecting that competition in a market has been distorted. Further, CCS has been empowered with the necessary powers to require the production of documents or information from relevant parties during market inquiries when the Competition Act was last amended.

Independent Appeal Mechanism

Appeals against CCS' determination are heard not by the Minister, but by a Competition Appeal Board (CAB). Modelled after the UK's Competition Appeal Tribunal, the CAB is an independent specialist tribunal appointed by the Minister. This framework was adopted as it was felt that CCS and CAB, being specialist bodies, would be better able to deal with their new area of law and facilitate the development of Competition Law. The CAB has 21 members headed by a chairman, who is a former Court of Appeal Judge. The Board also includes lawyers, economists, accountants, and representatives from the banking and business sectors.

Cross-Sectoral Cooperation

A number of sectors of the economy, such as the telecommunications, media, and energy sectors, are excluded from the Competition Act. These specific sectors are overseen by sector-specific regulators, who with their specialised technical knowledge and familiarity with the liberalisation and Competition Policy of their respective sectors are in a better position to oversee their specific sectors. Such an approach provides certainty to businesses and reduces compliance costs as businesses will not be subjected to two regulatory regimes.

For competition cases that are cross-sectoral in nature, CCS will work out with the relevant sector-specific regulators as to which regulator is best placed to handle the case, in accordance with the legal powers given to each regulator. This prevents double jeopardy and minimises the regulatory burden on businesses. CCS works in consultation with the regulators for this purpose in relation to the prohibitions against anti-competitive agreements, abuse of a dominant position, and mergers that substantially lessen competition.

CONCLUSION

Since its formation in 2005 and the commencement of the Competition Act in 2006, CCS has seen a wide range of cases come through its doors. Table 1 sets out the various categories of cases that CCS has commenced and concluded as of 30 November 2009.

Table 1: Case statistics: number of cases started and completed as of 30 November 2009.

Classification of cases	Cases started	Cases completed
Preliminary enquiries & investigations	56	42
Notification for guidance	10	5
Notification for decision	4	2
Mergers	15	15
Competition advisories	11	9

Chapter 6

HEALTHCARE: CONTAINING COST WITHOUT COMPROMISING QUALITY

Linda TAN Hui Min and CHEW Soon Beng

As many would know, Singapore is consistently ranked by the World Health Organization (WHO) and internationally regarded to be among the world's best in terms of healthcare delivery. This achievement is especially unique because her healthcare expenditure relative to her gross domestic product (GDP) is low compared to many developed countries.

The main findings of the chapter are that (1) Singapore has been able to contain the healthcare cost and yet not compromise its healthcare quality; (2) A large population, if not all, has access to quality healthcare without ballooning government expenditure on healthcare; and (3) The society at large has been involved in caring for the healthcare of the poor.

INTRODUCTION

A look at history and the media reports each day show that good, if not excellent, health is a universal desire of all human beings, yet not everyone can achieve this dream. Nonetheless, the tiny city-state of Singapore has fared well in building a healthy nation. According to the World Health Statistics 2009 published by the World Health Organization (WHO), she has an infant, child, and adult mortality rate of 2, 3, and 64 per 1,000 respectively. In addition, life expectancy at birth is at an astounding 81 years and healthy life expectancy at birth[1] is at 73 years. These results are commendable as these values are not only way above the median values of 71 and 62 years respectively, but also very close to the maximum values of 83 and 76 years too.[2]

In terms of supply of healthcare services, Singapore has 6,380 physicians, 18,710 nursing and midwifery personnel, and 1,190 dentistry personnel. This is equivalent to having 15 physicians, 44 nurses/midwives, and three dentists per 1,000 population respectively.[3] These surpass the global median values of 11 physicians, 29 nurses/midwives, and two dentists per 1,000 population and is comparable to values of some developed countries like United Arab Emirates and Republic of Korea.

With regard to hospital beds, there are 32 hospital beds per 10,000 population (WHO, 2009). Though a far cry from the maximum value of 140 beds per 10,000 population (achieved by Japan), it is comparable to other developed countries like Canada and the United States of America.

These statistics are not the only indicators of the success of the Singapore healthcare system. In its last World Health Report on health systems, Singapore was ranked top in Asia and sixth out of 191 countries by the WHO for our health system (WHO, 2000). Global consulting firm, Watson Wyatt, stated that "Singapore is generally acknowledged as having one of the most successful health care systems in the world, in terms of both efficiency in financing and the results achieved in community health outcomes" (Tucci, 2004).

[1] While life expectancy estimates reflect how many years a person might be expected to live, healthy life expectancy reflects how many years they might live in good health (WHO, 2009).

[2] Unless otherwise stated, all health indicators mentioned are obtained from the World Health Statistics 2009.

[3] Since life expectancy is more of an indicator for economic development, we also look at number of doctors per population, as well as waiting time for surgery (later) in order to better assess the quality of healthcare in Singapore.

The nation's success is also evident from many other international rankings[4] and quality care is further evident from the fact that the median waiting time for elective surgery is only one week. In fact, patients requiring emergency or urgent surgery are admitted immediately (WHO Regional Office for the Western Pacific, 2005).

These truly impressive achievements are made more extraordinary by the fact that the annual health expenditure in Singapore as a percentage of gross domestic product (GDP) is not even half that of many developed countries. To illustrate, the annual health expenditures in the USA, Denmark, UK, and Norway are 16%, 9.9%, 9%, and 8.6% of GDP respectively, but the annual health expenditure in Singapore is only 3.4% of GDP. It is worth mentioning that these Western countries have healthy life expectancies that are fairly close, if not identical, to that in Singapore. They stand at 78, 79, 80 and 81 years correspondingly.[5]

This chapter examines (1) how and why Singapore has been able to contain the cost and yet not compromise its healthcare quality; (2) how a large population has access to quality healthcare without ballooning government expenditure on healthcare; and (3) how the society at large is involved in caring for the healthcare of the poor.

Specifically, we first introduce the economic rationale for government intervention in the healthcare sector, then examine how healthcare cost is contained in the country. This is followed by a model illustrating the economics of our healthcare strategy, and finally, some concluding remarks.

---

[4] In 2003, Political and Economic Risk Consultancy (PERC) ranked Singapore's healthcare system as the third best in the world and the country best prepared to deal with a major medical crisis in Asia; in 2007, IMD's World Competitiveness Yearbook ranked Singapore's Health Infrastructure third out of 55 countries; and in 2008, Global Competitiveness Report ranked Singapore second for Infant Mortality Rate and twelfth for Life Expectancy at birth (81 years) (see http://www.moh.gov.sg/mohcorp/hcsystem.aspx?id=22966).

[5] Global Health Observatory Database. http://apps.who.int/ghodata/

GOVERNMENT INTERVENTION IN THEORY AND PRACTICE

Good health is not only coveted by individuals, but also by nations and governments as a healthy population implies a more productive workforce (which has larger economic implications such as on competitiveness and economic growth for instance) and fewer burdens on the state. Although the state of health has improved tremendously over the last few decades, increasing life expectancy and rising medical costs due to better technology have caused healthcare expenditures to increase both in terms of per capita as well as share of GDP for many countries. On the one hand, rising healthcare costs can hurt a country's competitiveness. On the other hand, how the healthcare delivery is financed between the state and the individuals can have an impact on the healthcare costs and individual health outcomes.

In economic theory, healthcare, like many other goods such as parks, education, and libraries, is a merit good which generates positive externalities[6] in consumption. This is because an individual who consumes healthcare services benefits not only himself, but also others as he is a more productive worker (thereby benefitting his firm) as well as less of a threat to others since there is reduced likelihood of others contracting a disease from him. The presence of these third-party benefits (also known as marginal external benefit or MEB) results in a divergence between marginal private benefit (MPB) and marginal social benefit (MSB) as shown in Fig. 1, with MSB > MPB.

As individuals take only their private costs and benefits into account in their decision making, the private outcome or equilibrium is at point A where MPB = MPC, where MPC is marginal private cost, and an amount of $0Q_p$ is consumed. However, the

[6] An externality is a cost or benefit arising from an economic transaction (i.e., production/consumption of a good or service) that falls on a third party and is not taken into account by those who undertake the transaction (i.e., buyers and sellers themselves). This is sometimes referred to as "spillover"/"third-party" costs or benefits.

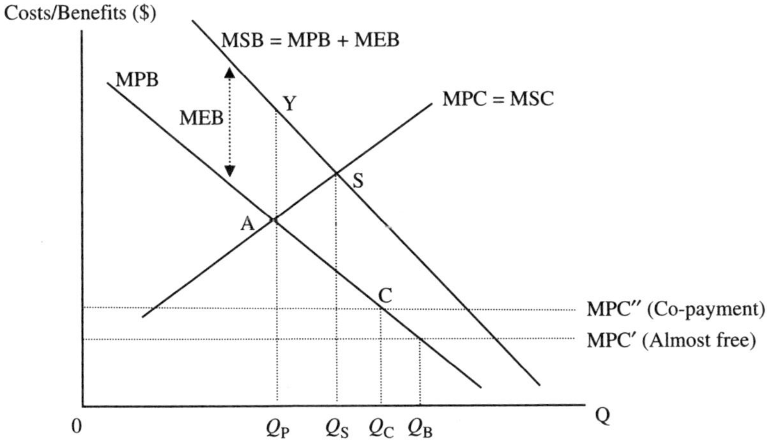

Fig. 1: Positive externalities in consumption.

socially optimal point is *S*, and the socially optimal level of consumption is Q_S, where MSB = MSC, where MSC is marginal social cost. Thus, when left to market forces, healthcare is under-consumed, and this leads society to incur a deadweight loss represented by the area ASY.

Under-consumption in the healthcare sector does not arise due to positive externalities alone. Other factors such as inequitable distribution of income (where the poor are unable to afford healthcare), imperfect knowledge (where consumers are ignorant of the benefits of healthcare), and market power (where private hospitals use their significant market power to raise prices or collude to charge higher prices) are some other reasons that could account for under-consumption. In any case, they provide ample justification for governments to intervene so as to bring the consumption level to a socially optimal one.

However, the issue in many developed countries is over-consumption due to the way healthcare is financed. If the government funding is big or there is third-party payment, MPC would be a low horizontal line given by MPC′. With the same MPB, MSB, and MSC, there is over-consumption of healthcare by the amount Q_SQ_B as these people covered by their respective governments or insurance consume at point B. In contrast, for those who are not covered, they under-consume (like in the case of developing countries) as their equilibrium is at point A.

The remedies to the issues of under-consumption and over-consumption are plenty. In the case of the former, the government can intervene through giving full or partial subsidies, providing the service themselves, or run campaigns and public education programmes to raise awareness of the benefits of healthy living and regular medical checkups. In the case of the latter, the government has to generally reduce the amount of subsidies given or have a co-payment philosophy.

Although some measures are better than others at solving the issue at hand, the key thing is that one has to shift from complete reliance on the price mechanism to allocate resources, to having some form of government intervention. The issue that arises is how much should be left to the state and how much should be left to free market forces. There is perhaps no consensus on this issue as statistics from the WHO show that there are varying degrees of state involvement for different countries, which of course, need not correlate directly with success.

In Singapore, only 33.6% of total expenditure on health is funded by general government expenditure, but this percentage goes as high as 45.8% for the US, 67.2% for Australia, 70.4% for Canada, 76.6% for Germany, 79.7% for France, 82.2% for Japan, and 87% for the UK.[7]

We can thus see that the Singapore government has played a relatively small role in the area of healthcare financing as compared to other countries. However, in terms of absolute amount, the Singapore government's health expenditure has been increasing over the years, as Table 1 indicates.

Such low public expenditure on healthcare (as % of GDP) could be achieved in Singapore due to the following reasons: (1) the dual healthcare delivery system ensures affordability and quality, (2) the design of the various healthcare financing schemes stresses a lot on

[7] WHO Statistical Information System, http://www.who.int/whosis/en/index.html.

Table 1: Singapore's government health expenditure.

	FY 02	FY 03	FY 04	FY 05	FY 06	FY 07	FY 08
Government health expenditure/ GDP (%)	1.0	1.2	0.9	N.A.	0.9	0.9	1.1
Government health expenditure/total government expenditure (%)	5.6	7.0	5.9	6.3	6.5	6.7	7.1
Government health expenditure per person (S$)	454	584	493	507	549	615	756

Source: Ministry of Health.

individual responsibility, and (3) there is a constant emphasis on healthy living and preventive healthcare programmes.

The benefits of such low public health expenditure are that it allows for low income and corporate tax rates for households and firms. This, in turn, enables the country to attract foreign talent and foreign investments which eventually act as sources of economic growth in our country. In the next section, we explain how the health-care cost is contained, but quality also maintained at a high level.

HEALTHCARE DELIVERY IN SINGAPORE

We discuss the healthcare system[8] in Singapore according to the following framework:

1. Restructuring of government hospitals
2. Provision of polyclinics
3. Provision of community hospitals
4. Role of CPF (Central Provident Fund) and healthcare insurance

[8] The focus in this paper is on public hospitals which mainly cater for a large segment of the population. The private hospitals are more for high-income citizens who are covered by private insurance and for foreign patients.

5. Role of employers
6. Medical subsidies for the poor
7. How doctors and hospitals are assessed
8. Investment in e-health record system
9. Healthy lifestyle
10. Economic strategy of containing healthcare cost without compromising quality.

Restructuring of Government Hospitals

As early as in 1980, the Singapore government was concerned that Singapore might follow the footsteps of advanced countries such as the USA in terms of rising healthcare costs if nothing was done. Thus Singapore has a dual system of healthcare delivery. The government manages the public system, while the private hospitals and general practitioners manage the private system. It goes without saying that the public system looks after the general population and the private system caters for high-income citizens and patients from abroad.

Despite the low public health expenditure, there is no lack of public-sector health facilities in Singapore. This is hardly surprising since the public system looks after the general population. As Table 2 indicates, the share of public-sector hospital beds stands at a whopping 71.8%, although this share has continuously declined from its value of 74.5% in 2003.

As patients are free to choose their providers within the dual healthcare delivery system, they can walk in for a consultation at any private clinic or any government polyclinic. To ensure that standards and patient safety are not compromised, the Ministry of Health (MOH) regulates all healthcare providers. This also helps to ensure that quality healthcare is provided in a cost-effective manner.

In Singapore, all levels of healthcare — primary, secondary, and tertiary specialist care — are easily accessible. The outpatient polyclinics and private medical practitioner's clinics provide primary healthcare, while the public and private hospitals provide secondary and tertiary specialist care.

In terms of the distribution between the public and private sectors, the public polyclinics provide 20% of the primary healthcare

Table 2: Statistics on health facilities in Singapore.

	2003	2004	2005	2006	2007	2008
Number of hospitals/ specialty centres	29	29	29	30	30	29
— Public sector	13	13	13	14	14	14
— Private sector	16	16	16	16	16	15
Total number of hospital beds	11,855	11,840	11,830	11,527	11,547	11,580
— Public-sector hospital beds	8,831	8,813	8,599	8,320	8,368	8,319
— Private-sector hospital beds	3,024	3,027	3,231	3,207	3,179	3,261
Number of polyclinics	17	17	18	18	18	18
Number of public-sector dental clinics	230	232	239	241	242	236

Source: Ministry of Health.

services while the private practitioners provide the remaining 80%. For hospital care, it is the reverse with 20% of hospital care being provided by the private sector and the remaining 80% by the public sector (see Table 3).

Of course, the healthcare system was not always like this. Prior to 1984, "medical services were provided mainly by the public sector and financed through general taxes. Medical services generally were provided free or at a nominal charge [and] the private sector played only a *modest* role" (Hsiao, 1995). However, corporatisation of public hospitals began in 1984 and it started with the National University Hospital.[9] Since then, "efforts to reform the public hospitals in Singapore have gone through three overlapping phases" (Ramesh, 2008).

The Singapore government restructured the government hospitals with the following objectives:

1. To minimise overlap of equipment and specialists (Hsiao, 1995).

[9] The experience was similar to the ones in the USA and UK under Reagan and Thatcher respectively.

Table 3: Singapore's healthcare delivery system.

	Primary healthcare	Secondary and Tertiary specialist care	Step-down care
Public sector	18 polyclinics (20%)	Seven restructured hospitals and six national centres (80%)	Community hospitals (welfare organisations)
Private sector	Private GP clinics (80%)	16 private hospitals (20%)	Private healthcare organisations

Source: Ministry of Health.

2. To allow hospitals to be more efficient by empowerment in the sense that hospitals are run by management committees and not by the Ministry of Health.
3. "To introduce 'accounting responsibility and commercial discipline' into hospital management and to improve the standard of hospital services and responsiveness to patients' needs" (Massaro and Wong, 1996). As the authors explained, "their newly created quasi-independent status presumably gives the hospitals greater entrepreneurial flexibility and allows them to respond rapidly to the changing marketplace."

The government tried to achieve these goals through the following means. As Hsiao (1995) describes, "the government separated financing from provision of hospital services by making public hospitals autonomous and financially independent." He further describes that they have a "fixed formula to subsidise hospital beds and do not take responsibility for the overall profit or loss of hospitals." This forces the public hospitals to raise quality and efficiency in order to maximise profits and not make losses.

Further to this, the government encouraged the private hospitals and clinics to develop and compete with those in the public sector. This reinforces the strategy mentioned above used to enhance quality and efficiency.

To ensure the private sector both competes and minimises costs, the government provided subsidies for public outpatient clinics and Class B1, B2, and C beds at public hospitals (Hsiao, 1995). In so doing, private-sector providers would have to remain competitive by minimising costs and offering higher-quality services. If not, they would not be able to vie with these subsidised services.

However, it is important to note that hospitals were given more operational autonomy and flexibility only in certain matters after corporatisation, such as in the areas of remuneration and human resource policy. Strategic oversight was still retained by the government as they continued to make decisions regarding board membership, regulations, and medical specialisation policy. Also, sensitive issues such as increases in fees continued to be under government purview so as to ensure that hospitals continue to carry out and fulfil their "social mission" to the people (Lim, 1998).

Nonetheless, Hsiao (1995) finds that "restructuring the public hospitals improved their efficiency. Productivity, as measured by the number of adjusted patient days per staffer, increased about 20%." A 1992 survey to gauge patients' opinions on the service of these hospitals, commissioned by restructured hospitals, showed that 90% of patients rated the services provided by the public hospitals as either good or excellent while 88% of the surveyed patients felt satisfied with the services and would recommend the hospitals to their relatives and friends.

In 2000, the government healthcare providers were re-organised into two clusters — National Healthcare Group and Singapore Health Services — each providing primary to tertiary care (see Appendix 1). The decision to cluster individual hospitals into two groups of hospitals came about because aggressive competition among individual hospitals obstructed good planning and optimal deployment of resources. Large and well-reputed hospitals made competition difficult for the smaller and less reputable ones. The government therefore announced the creation of two similarly sized "clusters" of public hospitals and clinics (Ramesh, 2008).

The move towards vertically integrated regional healthcare networks has intensified in recent years. There are now four healthcare

Table 4: Regional health networks in Singapore.

National Healthcare group	Singapore Health Services	National University Health System	Alexandra Health Pte Ltd
Tan Tock Seng Hospital Institute of Mental Health	Singapore General Hospital Changi General Hospital	National University Hospital National University — School of Medicine	Alexandra Hospital Jurong Medical Centre
National Skin Centre	KK Women's and Children's Hospital Singapore National Eye Centre National Heart Centre National Cancer Centre National Neuroscience Institute National Dental Centre		
Polyclinics in western part of Singapore	Polyclinics in eastern part of Singapore		

Source: Ministry of Health.
Note: Changes to the clustering ongoing, see http://www.moh.gov.sg/mohcorp/hcfacilities.aspx for the most updated information.

networks which consist of "restructured hospitals working in close partnership with other healthcare providers in the region, such as community hospitals, nursing homes, general practitioners, and home care providers" (Ho, 2009). Table 4 and Fig. 2 provide details on these collaborations.

This restructuring of the healthcare system reduces the need for services and resources to be duplicated across different care-settings, and allows the different clinical capabilities to be more optimally developed. It further enables better integrated and better quality healthcare services to be delivered through greater cooperation and collaboration among the different healthcare providers in each Regional Health System (RHS).

The way the public healthcare providers have been grouped together suggests that the restructuring was carefully designed

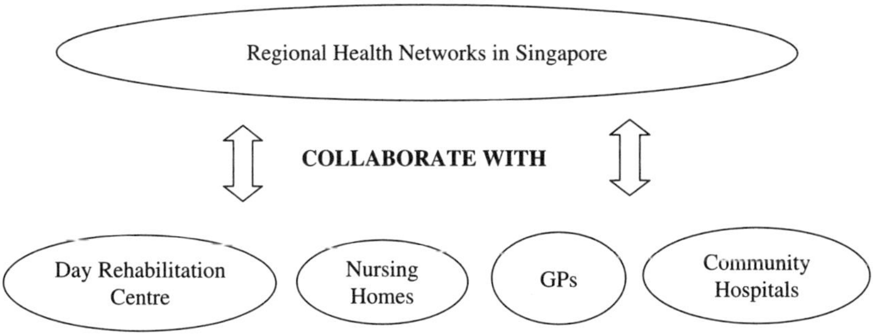

Fig. 2: Healthcare collaboration model.

based on both geographic and medical functional considerations. We can see that the above four groups or clusters are in different regions of Singapore, with the National University Health System in the far western end, Alexandra Health Pte Ltd in the western part, Singapore Health Services in the central/eastern portion, and National Healthcare Group in the central/western region.

This is hardly surprising as restructuring based on geographical factors allows the different health facilities to create and reap synergies more easily. This in turn helps to reduce costs and hence keep healthcare affordable for Singaporeans. It is also evident that the restructuring in government hospitals took into consideration each hospital's own niche areas and specialties. For instance, the National University Hospital is excellent for medical research, which is of course also a niche area of the National University School of Medicine.

Polyclinics

One of the smart things that Singapore has done is build polyclinics[10] for primary care. The Singapore government builds polyclinics nationwide to provide primary healthcare at low prices for citizens with

[10] Polyclinics are one-stop centers with (1) a multi-disciplinary team of health care professionals; (2) trained nurses who can take on additional roles such as health screening, patient counseling, and education; as well as (3) many facilities and services such as labs, pharmacy, and X-ray. Specifically, polyclinics provide primary

equally good quality. The polyclinics are well equipped with first-rate equipment and have well- and specially trained staff nurses. Patients generally see a doctor for the first visit. For subsequent visits to the polyclinic, the nurses who are trained for specific diseases can decide whether it is necessary to see the doctor again for the same treatment. The patient will pay less if he were to collect the same medicine without being examined by a doctor.

Community Hospitals

On community hospitals, the aim is to have one government hospital to one community hospital so that poor patients can move from the government hospital from which they were seeking treatment to a community hospital after operation. Some of these hospitals are funded by charities.

One good example is Ren Ci hospital, a community hospital. In 2006, the annual expenses came up to $16.69 million. With the government paying $8.80 million and the patients paying $1.29 million, this community hospital still runs a deficit of $6.60 million.[11] In order to continue looking after poor patients transferred from government hospitals, this community hospital has to raise funds from the public year after year.

Role of CPF and Healthcare Insurance

Having analysed the healthcare delivery system in Singapore, we look at healthcare financing in the following sections. The healthcare financing schemes in Singapore stress a lot on individual

---

acute and chronic outpatient care (they have programmes for chronic disease management, including conditions such as diabetes, etc., in addition to basic health screening, dietician services, minor surgical procedures, and travel health). Polyclinics also have Women and Children Clinics that look into women and children's health and immunisation; selected polyclinics provide other services such as ultrasound scans, dental services, and specialised services such as foot screening and psychiatric services.

[11] These figures are from the Ministry of Health.

responsibility, i.e., a lot of emphasis is placed on the individual to take care of their own healthcare expenses and meet their own healthcare needs. This approach will moderate the demand for healthcare consumption, and at the same time allow the government to have surplus funds to look after the poor.[12] Referring back to Fig. 1, the cost–benefit diagram shows that a co-payment system will shift up the horizontal supply curve from MPC′ to MPC″, reducing the amount of over-consumption by $Q_C Q_B$.

This indirectly helps to keep prices of healthcare affordable on top of the other supply-side measures undertaken by the government (e.g., making it a point to guard against a glut of expensive technology, lengthy hospital stays, and an excessive number of doctors and specialists). Figure 3 shows the breakdown of our healthcare financing system.

Let us examine each of these components in detail.

Medisave

Medisave is a national medical savings scheme introduced in April 1984 to help individuals build up their savings for healthcare

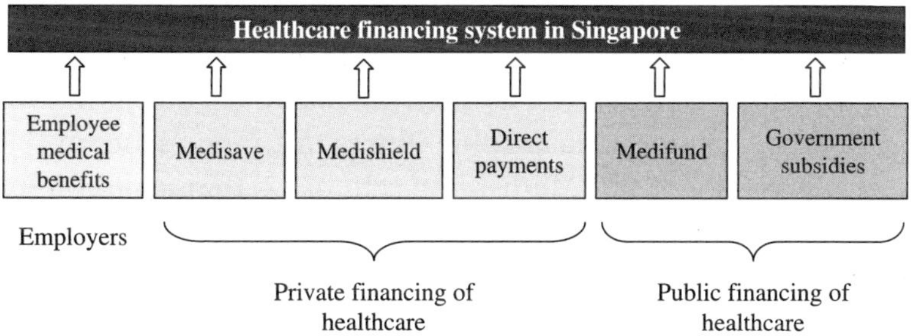

Fig. 3: Healthcare financing system in Singapore.

Source: Ministry of Health.

[12] In contrast, a free buffer approach in healthcare will create excessive demand for healthcare and ultimately the cost will be paid by the tax payers themselves and the healthcare sector characterised by low level of efficiency and poor accessibility.

purposes. Each month, every employee contributes a small percentage of his monthly salary to a personal Medisave account. The funds accumulated can be used for the account holder's personal or immediate family member's hospitalisation expenses.

The adoption of this national healthcare savings scheme implies a relatively low healthcare burden on the government since it is designed to stress individual responsibility. This translates to lower taxes in the economy as mentioned previously.

In addition, the government has placed caps on the amount withdrawn. This helps to ensure that the funds can be sustained over a long period of time and into old age. This is certainly an insightful move as well as a forward-looking measure as it helps to maintain long-term healthcare consumption.

Unfortunately, Medisave is only a savings account. Thus, one can easily wipe out one's Medisave balance if one incurs a very large medical bill, which is not uncommon these days, with escalating healthcare costs.

Medishield

To overcome the limitations of Medisave, the government introduced Medishield in 1990. Since it is designed to help members meet medical expenses from major or prolonged illnesses which cannot be sufficiently covered by their Medisave balance, Medishield is said to be a "low-cost catastrophic illness insurance scheme."[13]

The advantage of the Medishield scheme is that up to 80% of a large medical bill at the Class B2 or C ward can be covered by Medishield without huge expensive premiums.

Medifund

Medifund is a scheme to help needy Singaporeans who cannot pay their medical expenses. For more details about the scheme, please

[13] http://www.moh.gov.sg/mohcorp/hcfinancing.aspx?id=306

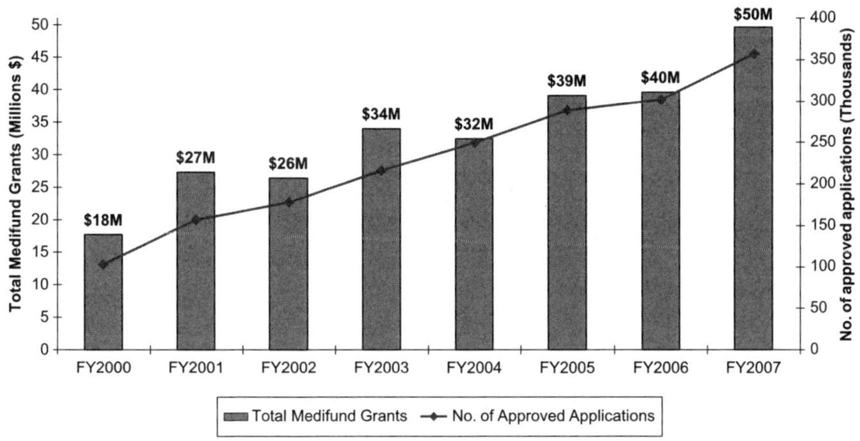

Fig. 4: Total Medifund grants and number of approved applications, 2000–2007. *Source*: Ministry of Health.

refer to the MOH website.[14] This scheme benefits the poor and those who really need help by giving them peace of mind. Nonetheless, the government set clear criteria as to who can qualify. For instance, the patient may be unemployed or retired but have assets or relatives who are able to help financially. It is clear from Fig. 4 above that the total Medifund grants and number of approved applications had been on a steady increase.

Role of Employers via Employee Medical Benefits

In addition to the schemes mentioned above, Singaporeans also make use of their employee medical benefits to finance their healthcare bills. Both the civil service and private sector offer these employee medical benefits, which help to alleviate the costs of healthcare in Singapore. Although the amount of medical benefits given differs between different employers, there is no doubt that this measure results in increased consumption of healthcare. The

[14] http://www.moh.gov.sg/mohcorp/hcfinancing.aspx?id=308

important thing is employees may be more productive due to increased healthcare consumption.

The challenge with this measure is that not all companies in the private sector will agree and follow the recommendations made. It is thus, a difficult measure to enforce as such benefits represent an additional cost to the employers and employees may also not want this option for fear of possible reduction in monetary wages. This measure also neglects the elderly and senior citizens in Singapore, which is perhaps the neediest group of all.

Government Medical Subsidies for the Poor

The government ensures that good and affordable healthcare is accessible to all through heavy government subsidies at the polyclinics and restructured hospitals. Tables 5A and 5B show the level of subsidies for polyclinics and restructured hospitals in 2008 compared to 1990.

These low charges at the hospitals and polyclinics are meant for low-income Singaporeans. Theoretically, the government should

Table 5A: Polyclinic fees/subsidy (1990 vs. 2008).

	Adult		Child/elderly	
Year	Subsidy level	Consultation fee	Subsidy level	Consultation fee
1990	NA	$6	NA	$3
2008	50%	$9	75%	$5

Table 5B: Hospital fees/subsidy (1990 vs. 2008).

		Ward class				
Year	Fee/subsidy	A1	A2	B1	B2	C
1990	Daily ward fee	$165	$135	$80	$28	$17
2008	Daily ward fee	$260–$295	$196–$220	$165–$180	$50–$60	$25–$30
	Subsidy level	0%	0%	20%	65%	80%

Source: Ministry of Health.

give a subsidy equivalent to the amount of MEB. This has the effect of raising the MPB to MSB (i.e., MPB′ = MSB), such that the private outcome is now at the socially optimal level.

From Fig. 1 and the above discussion, it is clear the government has made the right decision to offer only partial subsidies and not full subsidies for healthcare. This is because if the government decides to give full subsidies, there is bound to be over-consumption as the price falls to zero. This will imply longer queues, longer waiting lists, and longer waiting time. This is most detrimental as it crowds out available resources to those who really need it.

In addition, we note that the government offers different level of subsidies for different consumers. The merit of providing more subsidies for the elderly and children, and less for the adults at the polyclinics, is that it is more equitable than a general or flat subsidy for all. This is because the elderly and children generally do not have income and thus would require more financial help than a normal working adult. However, the scheme implemented at the polyclinics is not foolproof for there are children and senior citizens that come from relatively well-to-do or rich families who patronise these polyclinics in order to enjoy the low charges, and there are adults who have been unemployed for a long period of time.[15]

Since the government has provided different level of subsidies for different groups of consumers and allowed the use of Medisave for certain illnesses and treatments, the government may also consider providing different subsidies for different types of healthcare services. For example, the government should consider giving more subsidies to preventive healthcare treatments (e.g., vaccinations) as opposed to curative healthcare services or they can

[15] To check into the background of every patient at the polyclinic would be an administratively uphill task given the high volume. Thus to discriminate based on the group of consumers is perhaps the best thing to do. In fact, one must also note that this scenario, though possible, is not likely to occur. This is due to the relatively long waiting time at the polyclinics compared to the GPs, who charge reasonably too.

consider a particular range of healthcare services to be subsidised. For example, they may choose to subsidise basic or specific illnesses, but certainly not gout (commonly known as a rich man's disease).

With regard to subsidies at public hospitals, means testing has been introduced for public hospital patients starting from 1 January 2009. Under this scheme, the government will assess new patients' entitlement to subsidies for class B2 and C wards based on their tax-declared annual incomes or, for non-working patients, the annual value of their homes (Hospitals.SG, 2009). Thus, this is the most equitable scheme implemented to date and unlike the case of polyclinics, it is perhaps necessary to go to all this trouble for the case of hospitals considering the size of the subsidies involved.

How Doctors and Hospitals are Assessed and Remunerated

Fortunately, the subsidies and low charges at polyclinics and hospitals do not mean low wages for doctors working in these public facilities. If that were the case, large numbers of medical talents or choice specialists would leave the public sector for private institutions. When that happens, low income patients who cannot afford private medical care will not have the opportunity to consult the best doctors, and it would be difficult to groom the next generation of successors, as "institutional doctors who set their sights on future private practice may concentrate on honing their clinical skills at the expense of teaching and research (Lim, 2008). Thus, the "salary for public-sector doctors in Singapore (including bonuses, allowances, and staff benefits) is regularly reviewed and set competitively.[16] This helps to ensure that Singapore can attract the best talent and quality of care remains high in the public hospitals.

Among the different models available for the remuneration of healthcare providers, Singapore tries to find the middle ground. According to an article by SMU, most doctors are paid a base salary

---

[16] http://www.moh.gov.sg/mohcorp/careers.aspx?id=274#workenv.

Table 6: Representative salary scales.

Position	Base salary (S$Month)	Annual compensation w/bonuses and supplements	Exchange rate (Equivalent in US$)	PPP[a] (Equivalent in US$)
Junior nurse	1,500	22,000	14,200	17,000
Senior nurse	3,000	45,000	29,000	36,000
Senior registrar	7,000	105,000	68,000	84,000
Junior medical faculty	10,000	150,000	97,000	120,000
Senior medical faculty	13,000	195,000	126,000	166,000

Note: This table represents data based on the clinical faculty supplement option, which is normally lower than the incentive based on total billings. Thus these figures probably represent the lower range of salaries.

[a] Purchasing power parity.

Source: Ministry of Health.

that is set reasonably high, but there are additional dollars to be earned from seeing more patients (SMU, 2007, see Table 6). In addition, doctors in restructured hospitals are allowed to open their own private clinics. This helps to prevent doctors from leaving for the private sector. Massaro and Wong (1996) noted that in Singapore, "physicians earn five to six times the average wage, which is comparable to the United States."

E-Health Record System

However, the retention of good doctors is only necessary but not sufficient. The government has gone one step further, as the complexities of the healthcare continuum as mentioned earlier imply that the patients and their family members often struggle in making the right choices to meet their healthcare needs. For them to make a well-informed decision and for integrated healthcare to be delivered seamlessly, there has to be an "effective and efficient matchmaker" (Ho, 2009).

The Ministry of Health has set up the Agency for Integrated Care (AIC) for this purpose, that is, to help patients navigate the entire healthcare system and to help hospitals coordinate patient discharges from the restructured hospitals to the community hospitals and nursing homes (Ho, 2009).

Despite these efforts, there is currently still one slight glitch in this arrangement, and that is the various healthcare providers do not have shared access to relevant medical records. Since only restructured hospitals and polyclinics are currently on the electronic medical records exchange (EMRX), the other parties following up on the same patient (like GPs and private hospitals) do not have access to the key medical data relevant to the patient's treatment. Towards this end, MOH is working towards an Electronic Health Record[17] (EHR) for the entire nation.[18]

Actualising this goal of having "One Patient, One Medical Record" will cut down the time and expenses incurred by patients as they no longer need to repeat their medical history and undergo the same tests each time they visit a different doctor (Ho, 2009). According to executives from GE Healthcare, Singapore stands in good stead for the successful implementation of these e-healthcare initiatives.

It is clear from the above discussion that the delivery system will continue to evolve and the healthcare landscape will be dramatically different in no time to come. With the e-health record system, fewer tests will be conducted and less time will be wasted. This is in line with reducing the healthcare cost without reducing healthcare outcome.

Healthy Lifestyle

The last item, a healthy lifestyle, is a forward-looking preventive measure and thus is perhaps the best. Singaporeans are encouraged

---

[17] The EHR will "capture patient data in a single record and allow appropriate access by medical personnel from different entities" (Yeo, 2009).

[18] There are plans for the EHR to be ready by November 2010, with participation initially from a pool of public hospitals, community hospitals and general practitioners and for an integrated national EHR system by 2014 (Yeo, 2009).

to adopt a healthy lifestyle and be actively responsible for their own health. They are often reminded of the adverse effects of harmful habits like smoking, and the importance of regular exercise, balanced diets, stress management, etc. through public education and outreach programmes. These programmes target not only adults, but also school-going children and teens, as evident from the fact that many of these programmes and initiatives are rolled out in schools. This helps to cultivate in our children the habit of living a healthy lifestyle (from a young age). Examples of such programmes include dedicated (i.e., a restricted number of) fried food days, annual National Physical Fitness Assessment (NAPFA) tests, yearly All Children Exercise Simultaneously (ACES) Day, and active promotion of Co-Curricular Activities (CCAs).

Economic Healthcare Strategy

In Fig. 5, ABCDE is a typical demand curve for healthcare consumption by a patient. He needs to see a doctor for primary care (AB), follow this up with an operation (CD), and then needs to recuperate (DE). If all these are done at a hospital (either paid for by him (a rich man), or by an insurance company or by the government), the total healthcare bill is 0GIE. This is a main reason why, in many countries with generous support from the government, the healthcare cost as a proportion of their GDP can be as high as 10%.

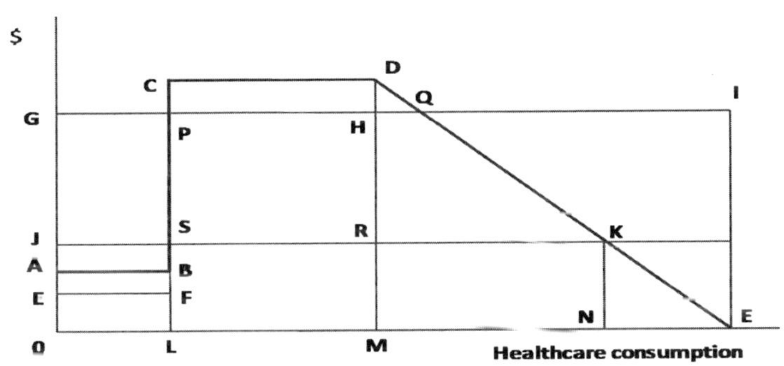

Fig. 5: Demand curve for healthcare consumption.

And a large portion of the medical expenses is wasted, which is area AGPB + area QIE. This type of blind healthcare subsidy will hurt the competitiveness of the countries in terms of higher labour costs and higher income tax rates.

In Singapore, as mentioned above, the method most commonly adopted by patients is to first go to a polyclinic for primary care, then to a government hospital for operation, and finally, to a community hospital for recuperating, especially for low-income citizens.

Assuming that there is constant cost per day or per service and that the horizontal distances EF, PH, and RK represent the cost of healthcare/treatment at the polyclinics, hospitals, and community hospitals respectively, the total cost incurred by the society is area 0EFPHRPE (area 0EFL + area LPHM + area MRPE). The consumer surplus is equal to area EABF + PCDH + area RDQK, but the dead weight loss is area KPE as poor patients have nowhere to go but stay at the community centre. Hence, area OEFPHRPE is Singapore's healthcare expenditure which is about 3% of her GDP, and this is achieved without reducing healthcare consumption. The government of Singapore pays less than this amount because there will be not much subsidy for high-income Singaporeans using the polyclinics and government hospitals. Furthermore, the government of Singapore only pays half of the cost at community hospitals; the other half is paid for by charity organisations.

The benefits of this strategy extend beyond the realm of economics. The advantages gained are not restricted to cost savings and consumer surplus alone. To illustrate, a patient can now recuperate at Ren Ci Community Hospital after being discharged from Tan Tock Seng Hospital instead of being sent directly home. This arrangement clearly facilitates his recovery (and reduce the frustrations at home) as his family members, who are not trained caregivers, may not have the necessary skills and expertise to tend to him. He can further enjoy continuity of care after his stay at Ren Ci Community Hospital through services like day rehabilitation centres, home nursing, GP follow ups and so on (Ho, 2009). Thus a patient no longer has to worry about where to get continued care and support upon his discharge from an acute hospital.

CONCLUSION

This chapter has examined Singapore's healthcare strategy, and we hope that the chapter provides insights into how governments can better manage their healthcare systems to have a healthy population. Singapore's healthcare strategy can be summarised as follows: The healthcare system operates efficiently: avoid duplicated equipments or tests; encourage healthy competition among hospitals; advertise operation charges; invest in e-medical record systems. Hospitals are meant to treat serious illness and perform operations. Primary medical care is the responsibility of private clinics and for the poor, they can go to polyclinics. For the poor, they are admitted to community hospitals for step-down care meaning to recuperate after the operation. The average citizens must buy healthcare insurance. The poor will be assisted by the government in terms of subsidies. Different subsidies are meant for different hospital wards and different income groups. Community hospitals are basically funded by charities but the government does subsidise low income patients.

REFERENCES

Global Health Observatory Database, http://apps.who.int/ghodata/

Ho, H.K. (2009) Transforming Healthcare Delivery in Singapore. *SMA News*, October.

Hospitals.SG. (2009) Singapore starts means testing in hospitals. *Hospitals SG*, 8 January, http://www.hospitals.sg/singapore-starts-means-testing-hospitals

Hsiao, W. (1995) Medical savings accounts: Lessons from Singapore. *Health Affairs*, 14(2), 260–266.

Lim, M.K. (1998) Health care systems in transition II. Singapore, Part I. An Overview of Health Care Systems in Singapore. *Journal of Public Health Medicine*, 20(1), 16–22.

Massaro, T. and Wong, Y.N. (1996) Medical Savings Accounts: The Singapore Experience, The National Center for Policy Analysis, Policy Report No. 203.

Ministry of Health Statistical Database, www.moh.gov.sg

Ramesh, M. (2008) Autonomy and control in public hospital reforms in Singapore. *The American Review of Public Administration*, 38(1), 62–79.

SMU (2007) The business of healthcare: A slippery slope. *Knowledge@SMU*, 3 October 03, http://knowledge.smu.edu.sg/article.cfm?articleid=1098

Tucci, J. (2004) The Singapore health system – achieving positive health outcomes with low expenditure. *Watson Wyatt Healthcare Market Review*, http://www.watsonwyatt.com/europe/pubs/healthcare/render2.asp?ID=13850

WHO (2009) *World Health Statistics 2009*. Geneva: World Health Organization, p. 43

WHO (2000) *The World Health Report 2000: Health Systems, Improving Performance*. Geneva: World Health Organization, http://www.who.int/whr/2000/en/

WHO Regional Office for the Western Pacific (2005) Health Situation in Singapore, *Country Health Information Profiles*. WHO Regional Office for the Western Pacific, http://www.wpro.who.int/countries/2005/sin/health_situation.htm

Yeo, V. (2009) S'pore e-health records roadmap 'pragmatic', ZDNet Asia, 30 October, http://www.zdnetasia.com/s-pore-e-health-records-roadmap-pragmatic-62058989.htm

APPENDIX 1

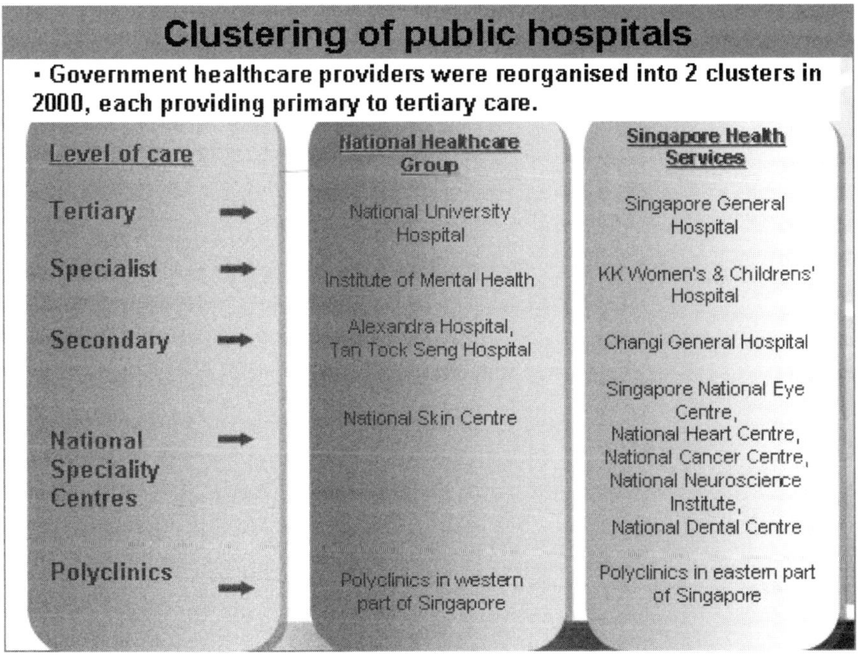

Source: Ministry of Health.

Chapter 7

ECONOMICS OF TRAINING: MARKET FAILURE AND GOVERNMENT INTERVENTION

Rosalind CHEW

Market failure in training often takes place because of employee poaching and job-hopping. Because of this, the government must step in to encourage employers to train their workers. Also, to prevent the low-wage poverty trap that youth workers tend to fall into, the government must step in to provide effective vocational training. The chapter shows how Singapore prevents market failure in training and the potential poverty trap that confronts youth workers, by providing a web of training programmes which practically covers all of Singapore's workers.

This chapter examines market failure with regard to training in three areas. First, the chapter shows why employers are reluctant to train their employees and how Singapore has been able to overcome such resistance. The second and third areas of market failure concern older workers and youth workers.

Market failure in training often takes place because the likelihood of employee poaching and job-hopping deprive employers of the skills of employees, and erodes the returns to their investment in the training of their employees. Furthermore, in any society, there are the generally older and lowly educated low-income workers who lack the initiative to seek assistance for skills training. Hence, they must be identified and persuaded to take part in training. At the same time, academically poor students who may not have completed secondary schools are forced to work as youth workers. Due to their lack of skills, these youth workers earn low wages. These youth workers, if they do get married, are likely to have low family earnings. Their children generally would not do well in school and may be trapped in the poverty cycle. The chapter argues that the government must find ways to provide effective vocational training to these youth so that such youth can earn a good family wage and thus escape the poverty cycle. The chapter shows how Singapore prevents this potential problem by providing effective vocational education.

The chapter also briefly examines training schemes in Korea, China, and the USA.

MARKET FAILURE

The training of workers may be undertaken by employers, especially if the required skills are specific to the needs of the firm (for a formal discussion on this topic, see Borjas, 2010). However, employers are often not willing to train their workers because workers may resign after training, which would prevent the employers enjoying a return on their investment in the workers' training. This results in market failure if most employers do not want to train workers but would rather poach trained workers from other employers, with the consequence that few workers would receive training in the economy.

Figure 1 depicts the impact of training on worker productivity. It shows that a typical worker without training earns $1,000 if his value of marginal product (VMP) is $1,000 per period. If he receives training while at work, his VMP during the training period (between period 0 and 1) is only $600 for example. In this case, the cost of training to the employer is $400. After completing his training, the VMP of this worker rises to, say, $1,400 per period. Hence, from the society's point of view, the rate of return on this training programme is positive.

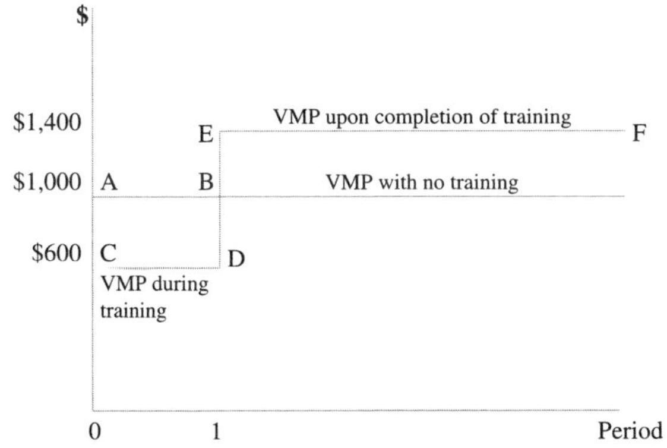

Fig. 1: The impact of training on worker productivity.

Generally, workers would not want to suffer a reduction in take-home pay to attend a training programme. Hence, they would insist on being paid $1,000 during the training period. The employer may be willing to bear the cost of training the workers if he can continue to pay the worker $1,000 after the training period. However, since the worker's market value after training is $1,400 per period, other firms can poach this worker as they can offer this trained worker a wage rate up to $1,400 per period. Firms know that it is more profitable to poach than to train. Consequently, few firms would train workers in the economy.

If there is sufficient communication between the firm and the worker, both can agree to share the cost of training. For example, during the training period, the worker may agree to receive $*J* in wages, which means he will bear a cost equal to his foregone earnings during training (i.e., the difference between VMP without training and his wage during training, $1,000 – $*J*) and that the employer will bear a cost of $*J* – $600 during this period (Fig. 2). After training, the worker's wage is set at $*K* for the first post-training period and at $1,400 thereafter. Hence total training cost for the employer would be ($*J* – $600) – ($1,400 – $*K*). Few trained workers will be poached in this case, because the incentive to leave is not as strong now.

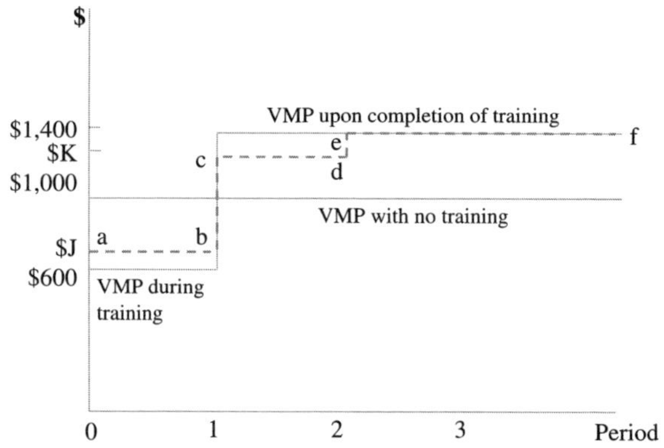

Fig. 2: Employer and worker share the cost of training. The wage line with shared training cost is the broken line abcdef.

In practice, employers may not want to train their workers, as the sharing of cost between the worker and the employer may be too complex and costly. Furthermore, even if the employer were willing to share the cost of training with the worker, the worker may be still be unwilling to undergo training because of the opportunity cost of the reduced pay due to his lower VMP during the training period. Consequently, if the government does not intervene, the number of workers receiving training may be too small, and the labour market and the economy would not be competitive.

SOLVING THE PROBLEM OF MARKET FAILURE

To overcome market failure in training, governments may want to find ways to encourage firms to train workers. Imposing a levy is a common way to force firms to train workers. In Singapore, for example, the Skills Development Fund (SDF) was set up in 1979 (see Lim, 1984 for a discussion on the SDF) to facilitate the training of employees. All firms in the private sector are required to pay an SDF levy. It is a tax on the payroll and is a sunk cost.

Under the SDF scheme, the SDF takes over the worker's cost during training of (\$1,000 – \$*J*) while the employer bears the

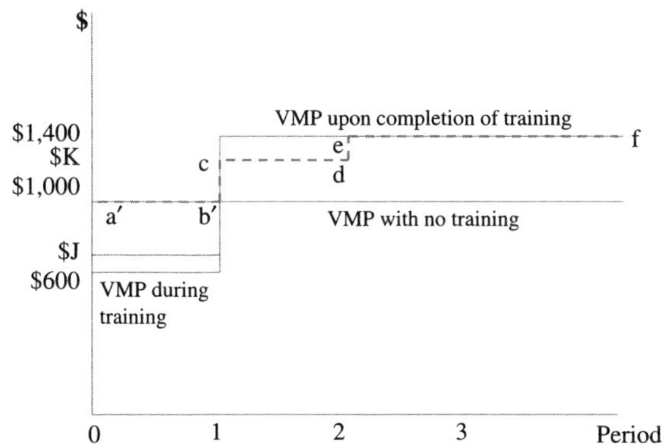

Fig. 3: How SDF solves market failure. The wage line under the SDF scheme is the broken line a′ b′ cdef.

difference between $*J* and the worker's lower VMP during training, $*J* – $600. Hence, the worker does not have to bear any cost at all during the training period. That is, he does not have to suffer a pay reduction to $*J* but continues to receive a wage equal to his VMP without training (i.e., $1,000, Fig. 3). The employer is released from having to work out a complex cost-sharing scheme with the worker. Upon completion of the training, the employer recoups his investment by paying the worker $*K* (which is less than the worker's VMP after training) for the first post-training period and at $1,400 thereafter. Moreover, the incentive for the worker to undergo training is very much greater under the SDF scheme.

In certain parts of China, firms are required to set aside a budget for training, but unlike the SDF levy, this fund is retained by the firms. The provincial government has to check whether the fund is still there and whether the funds are being used for training. Firms do not have the incentive to train their workers under this arrangement, as they still keep the money, and sometimes they use the funds for purposes other than training. The administrative cost of monitoring the usage of this fund is very high.

In Korea, firms pay a levy if they do not train their workers (Chew and Chew, 1999). Some firms, such as those in Norway, find that it is cheaper to pay a levy than to train their workers (Raaum and Hege, 2002).

THE SDF

As stated above, in Singapore, all firms in the private sector are required to pay an SDF levy. The SDF levy collected is used to subsidise the training of workers in Singapore on a co-payment basis.

At present, firms are required to pay 0.25% of their total wage bill to the SDF. All firms can apply to the SDF for a subsidy for the training of their workers. Under the SDF scheme, firms are expected to choose their own training programmes for their workers. They can enjoy a subsidy of up to 70% of the training cost, which means that firms have to pay at least 30% of the training cost. This ensures that the training programme that is selected is what the firm desires. An additional criterion for receiving an SDF subsidy is that trainees must achieve at least 75% attendance rate. Furthermore, trainees must sit for all examinations if the course leads to certification.

There are three shortcomings of the SDF:

1. The SDF cannot take care of the unemployed;
2. Small and medium enterprises (SMEs) are not keen to make use of SDF funds to train their workers; and
3. The SDF cannot take care of workers who want to change jobs (employers).

These shortcomings are resolved with the introduction of the Singapore Workforce Development Agency (WDA), which has specific training programmes for the unemployed and for workers from SMEs (see Regnér, 2002 for a discussion on the training of the unemployed in Sweden). WDA also provides assistance to professionals to switch professions under the Professional Skills Programme (PSP). It also runs the Job Re-creation Programme (JRP) to convert low-paying jobs to better-paying jobs. JRP also converts jobs held by foreign workers to jobs for local workers by means of upgrading the quality and responsibility of the jobs.

During the recent recessions, the SPUR (Skills Programme for Upgrading and Resilience) scheme was introduced. Training support under SPUR is, at 90%, higher than under the SDF scheme. Furthermore, SPUR pays 90% of absentee payroll during the training period, in addition to the 90% of the training cost. SPUR is fully funded by the government. This scheme is operational only during periods of recession.

TRAINING OF OLDER WORKERS IN THE INFORMAL SECTOR

Both SDF and WDA cover the training of workers in the formal sector, but not workers in the informal sector. The latter are low wage earners and lowly educated; they would not seek assistance on their own initiative. In the early 1990s, the Singapore government set up self-help bodies along racial groupings to provide assistance for such workers and their families. It is felt that these workers would respond well if the assistance comes from their respective communities. In this chapter, the Chinese Development Assistance Council (CDAC) is used as an example to show the importance of training.

The CDAC helps the children of low-income Chinese workers by providing them with free tuition. More importantly, the CDAC encourages these low-income Chinese workers to accept training in various programmes so that they can be enabled to hold on to a stable job. The CDAC motivates these low-income workers to accept and complete a training programme, not only by subsidising the training programme, but also by offering participants who complete any training programme a cash reward to further offset their training costs. The cash reward not only gives these workers the incentive to complete their training programme, but also reduces the cost of training to these workers to a very affordable nominal sum.

TRAINING OF YOUTH WORKERS

Youth workers generally refer to the academically less inclined school leavers and school dropouts. If no concerted effort is made to induce youth workers to take up vocational education when they are still young, later in life they will become poor working adults (Lynch, 1992). Governments of most countries wish to minimise youth unemployment. Many governments attempt to do this by finding work for them. This is a second-best solution. The best solution is not to push them into the job market, but to provide them with effective vocational education to enable them to earn a living throughout their lifetime (Chew and Chew, 2010). The important question is deciding on the form of vocational education for the academically less inclined school leavers and school dropouts.

Apprenticeship is a system of training a new generation of practitioners of a skill. Apprentices (or in early modern usage "prentices") or protégés build their careers from apprenticeships. Most of their training is done on the job while working for an employer who helps the apprentices learn their trade, in exchange for their continuing labour for an agreed period after they become skilled. Theoretical education may also be involved, informally via the workplace and/or by attending vocational schools while still being paid by the employer. Members of the Pennsylvania Apprentice Coordinators Association in the USA, for instance, have provided information on their website to help an individual decide if he/she has the aptitude and ability to train for a career in the construction industry.

In Germany, apprenticeships are part of Germany's dual education system, and as such form an integral part of many people's working life in that country. Finding employment without having completed an apprenticeship is almost impossible for occupations such as doctor's assistants, dispensing opticians, plumbers, and oven builders. In many countries, the government provides tax breaks for firms that provide apprenticeships. An apprenticeship is similar to a closed shop union in the sense that one has to be a member before you can apply for a job in a certain industry.

Figure 4 shows the impact of apprenticeship on the earnings of youth workers. Without training, youth will earn a low wage, along the line gh. Under apprenticeship, the youth's VMP is even lower, at ef, and he is paid even less than that, at ab. The firm providing the apprenticeship gets a VMP of ef and pays ab in wages.

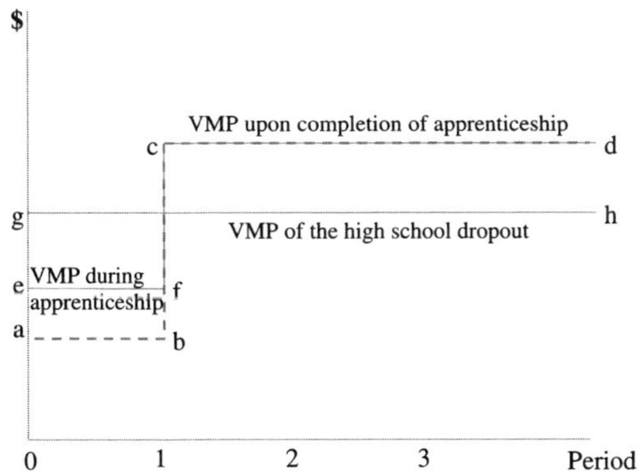

Fig. 4: The wage line of the youth worker with apprenticeship. The wage line is the broken line abcd.

The government pays for the difference in VMP as part of the cost of training. Firms employing graduates of apprenticeship schemes pay a wage equal to the graduate's VMP, along the wage line cd, which contributes to a respectable family wage.

Many countries also conduct effective training programmes for their youth. In the USA, the Local Workforce Development Board (LWDB) pays participants a wage during training and also pays employers for conducting the training. Employers who do not really train the workers will be blacklisted by the LWDB. The administrative cost of the LWDB is not low. (Unfortunately, no data on number of trainees by the LWDB are available.) It goes without saying that the total cost of training borne by the LWDB can be higher than the monthly VMP of the trainee.

INSTITUTE OF TECHNICAL EDUCATION, ITE

In the case of Singapore, students who do not do very well in their O-level exams join the ITE for an effective vocational education, with which ITE graduates are able to earn good wages (see Chew and Chew, 2010 for Singapore's public policy on vocational education). For some of the courses, ITE graduates are awarded professional certificates in addition to the ITE certificates. For instance, ITE has inked an MOU with Adobe, a leading software development agency, under which Adobe awards certification for courses in Digital Media Design, Digital Audio, and Video Production and Multimedia Technology for students as well as for faculty members. ITE graduates in these courses will receive the Adobe Certificate Associates (ACA) certification in addition to the ITE certificate.

Although training provided by Adobe is expensive, the returns are long term. ITE's cooperation with Adobe certification is a good business model for vocational education.

CONCLUSION

Competition among nations boils down to which countries can conduct more effective training programmes for their workers. If they fail to train their workers, the society subsequently will have to pay more in terms of welfare and retrenchment benefits, etc. This applies to workers in the formal sector as well as to those in the informal sector. There is no free lunch, and prevention is better than the cure.

There is a Chinese proverb by Lao Tze which says, "Give a man a fish, and you feed him for a day. Teach a man to fish, and you feed him for a lifetime". Hence, training and re-training is the key to providing workers with a lifelong income, via continued employment, not necessarily in the same occupation or with the same employer. The Singapore experience shows that the best form of training is to train workers before they are retrenched. This has been the focus of the SDF. Once they are retrenched, a system must be in place to train them and to help them to move on to another occupation. This has been the focus of the WDA. Low-income workers in the informal sector have to be motivated to accept and complete training programmes. This has been the focus of the CDAC and other self-help bodies. Those who do not do well in the O-level exams have to be provided with a holistic approach to effective vocational education so that these academically inadequate youth can be gainfully employed and can have the benefit of a respectable family income. This has been the focus of the ITE. Furthermore, there is a web of training schemes for those who leave formal schooling at various stages to catch up and move back into the mainstream of employment (see Chew and Chew, 2010 for these training and education programmes).

Thus, there is in Singapore a web of training programmes which practically covers all of Singapore's workers, because the Singapore government places a great deal of emphasis on the training of workers. In fact, SDF, WDA, CDAC, and training programmes organised by National Trades Union Congress together account for the training of about 400,000 workers each year (Chew and Chew, 2010). This implies that, with a local workforce of 1.6 million persons, each local worker is trained once every four years.

REFERENCES

Borjas, G. (2010). *Labor Economics*, 5th Ed., New York: McGraw-Hill.

Chew, Soon Beng and Rosalind Chew (1999). Human capital formation through on-the-job training in East Asia. In *Human Capital Formation as an Engine of Growth: The East Asian Experience*, pp. 173–202. Singapore: Institute of Southeast Asian Studies.

Chew, Soon Beng and Rosalind Chew (2010). Youth employment and training in Singapore. *Bulletin of Comparative Labour Relations* 73, 119–132.

Lim, Chong Yah (1984). *Economic Restructuring in Singapore.* Singapore: Federal Publications.

Lynch, Lisa, M. (1992). Private-sector training and the earnings of young workers. *American Economic Review* 82(1), 299–312.

Raaum, Oddbjorn and Torp, Hege (2002). Labour market training in Norway — effect on earnings. *Labour Economics* 9, 207–247.

Regnér, Håkan (2002). A nonexperimental evaluation of training programs for the unemployed in Sweden. *Labour Economics* 9, 187–206.

Chapter 8

A REVIEW OF THE US-SINGAPORE FREE TRADE AGREEMENT*

CHEE Yoke Heong and CHIA Wai Mun

Among all the countries in Asia, Singapore was one of the earliest and most active countries which pursued the path of bilateralism as a major instrument of its commercial trade strategy, by engaging in free-trade agreements (FTAs) with its trading partners around the world. It was the first in the region to sign an FTA with the USA. This study attempts to provide a general overview of Singapore's trade policy in relation to its move towards bilateral and regional FTAs. It focuses on the USSFTA and its effects after five years, with a view of drawing some lessons from Singapore's experience with the world's largest economy.

INTRODUCTION

Bilateral and regional trade agreements have taken off in a major way around the world, and Asia as a region is in the forefront of free-trade agreement (FTA) activity having the most number of agreements either concluded or in the pipeline compared to

* This study was conducted under the Asia Journalism Fellowship 2010 programme sponsored by the Nanyang Technological University (NTU) and Temasek Foundation in Singapore. Special thanks to Xie Taojun, Dou Liyu, and Li Mengling for their help in gathering the statistical data.

the other regions. Among all countries in the region, Singapore was one of the earliest and most active countries which pursued the bilateralism path as a major instrument of its commercial trade strategy, by engaging in FTAs with its trading partners around the world. It was the first in the region to sign an FTA with the USA, and the FTA is often regarded as a model of a successful agreement as the USA's attempts with a number of other Asian countries, namely South Korea, Thailand, and Malaysia, remained unfulfilled. The US–Singapore FTA (USSFTA) which came into effect in January 2004 is also significant in terms of scope. It encompasses provisions that are often not part of conventional bilateral trade agreements such as intellectual property rights, investment, government procurement, labour, and environment, most of which are topics that are not covered or discussed in the World Trade Organisation (WTO). For both countries, the FTA was motivated by economic and strategic interests.

This study attempts to provide a general overview of Singapore's trade policy in relation to its move towards bilateral and regional FTAs. It focuses on the USSFTA and its effects after five years, with a view of drawing some lessons from Singapore's experience with the world's largest economy.

RATIONALE AND DEVELOPMENT OF USSFTA

Singapore is one of the closest allies of the USA in Southeast Asia, and both countries share strong trade and security relations. Given the excessive volume of annual trade in goods and services between the two countries and foreign direct investment of the USA to Singapore, the USSFTA is of great interest to major companies and would be by far the largest outside of NAFTA (North American Free Trade Agreement) (Feinberg, 2006).

Though Singapore subscribes to free trade and multi-lateralism to safeguard and ensure a free and open international trading environment, it is also conscious of the global political economy issues and difficulties (Low, 2006). The decision to enter into FTA negotiations with the USA is part of the trend towards bilateralism and regionalism stemmed from a combination of reasons including the dismal prospects for progress in liberalisation at the international and regional levels. To some observers (Desker, 2004), the bilateral and regional route was a pragmatic decision, given the frustration over the multi-lateral process even though it is a second-best option over multi-lateral trade liberalisation. While Singapore increasingly favours bilateral and regional FTAs, it employs a multi-pronged strategy and continues to support the WTO process. By April 2010, Singapore has completed 20 agreements, six under negotiations while seven have been proposed as summarised in Table 1, making it by far the most active Asian economy in terms of the number and geographic coverage of FTAs.

The actual proposal for the FTA between the USA and Singapore was first brought up during discussions between the then Singapore Prime Minister Goh Chok Tong and the former US President Bill Clinton in 2000 during the Asia-Pacific Economic Cooperation (APEC) summit in Brunei. This was followed by the first round of talks two weeks later. Subsequent rounds of meetings were held to hammer out the details of the agreement, and after much tensions and differences over some contentious issues, an agreement was reached in December 2003 (Koh and Chang, 2004; Dent, 2006).

Both the economic and strategic motivations are played out in the USSFTA. Though Singapore has a robust trade relation with the USA, since 1997, trade between the USA and Singapore has steadily decreased, and by 2001 Malaysia overtook the USA as Singapore's number one trading partner. This trend continued into 2002 when trade fell by $6.9 billion. The Singapore government was hoping to reverse the trend and to gain loss ground when the effects of the USSFTA materialises (Lee, 2006). On the strategic front, Singapore's chief negotiator to the USSFTA, Tommy Koh, made clear that the FTA is far from just securing tariff-free entry of Singapore's exports to the US market or attracting FDI to the republic. It is to entrench the presence of the USA in the region because it underpins the security of the whole Asia-Pacific region (Koh and Chang, 2004). The September 11

Table 1: List of Singapore's FTAs.

Concluded	Under negotiations	Proposed/under consultation/study
ASEAN Free-Trade area (1993)	ASEAN-EU (2007)	Chile
ASEAN-Australia-New Zealand (2010)	Canada (2002)	Comprehensive Economic East Asia Free-Trade (ASEAN+3)
ASEAN-China (2010)	Egypt (2006)	Economic Partnership for East Asia (CEPEA/ASEAN+6)
ASEAN-India (2010)	Mexico (2000)	Morocco
ASEAN-Japan (2009)	Pakistan (2005)	South African Customs Union (SACU)
ASEAN-Korea (2007)	Ukraine (2007)	Sri Lanka
Australia (2003)		Taipei, China
China (2009)		
Costa Rica (2010)		
Gulf Cooperation Council (2008)		
India (2005)		
Japan (2002)		
Jordan (2005)		
Korea (2006)		
New Zealand (2001)		
Peru (2009)		
Panama (2006)		
Trans-Pacific Strategic Economic Partnership Agreement (2006)		
The United States (2004)		
European Free-Trade Association–Singapore FTA (2003)		

Source: Ministry of Trade and Industry; ADB FTA database; Kawai (2007).

terrorist attack in the USA added a new strategic dimension to the USSFTA process which led some observers to believe that Singapore's strong support for the former US President George Bush administration's stance on terrorism and the Iraq war speeded up the USSFTA project over other FTAs the USA was involved with (Dent, 2006).

For the USA, Singapore is also important economically and strategically. The USA is Singapore's largest foreign direct investor, while Singapore is the second largest Asian investor in the USA after Japan. Also an FTA with Singapore could serve as a template and set the standard for the USA in its negotiations with other Asian countries and for it to further strengthen its foothold in the region.

SINGAPORE-US FTA — FIVE YEARS ON

This section aims to provide a general assessment of the US–Singapore FTA since it came into effect in January 2004 by focusing on selected key economic impacts of the FTA.[1]

Trade in Goods and Services

Merchandise trade

The USSFTA has over the years increased the trade between the two countries as the volume of merchandise trade has consistently shown an upward trend as shown in Fig. 1. This may suggest that though Singapore has generally operated on a free-trade mode, the FTA has further opened up markets in Singapore to the USA. Though exports from Singapore to the USA have increased steadily since 2003, it has been at a rate slower than imports. Prior to the FTA, Singapore recorded a merchandise trade deficit of S$1.1 billion in 2003 with the USA, but this figure ballooned to $12.7 billion in 2008.

Singapore's exports to the USA

Despite the increase in trade and the USA being a major export destination for Singapore, its importance, as summarised in Table 2,

[1] Some of the statistical data in this section are adapted and updated based on an earlier report prepared by the US Congressional Research Service on the effects of the USSFTA three years after (http://fas.org/sgp/crs/row/RL34315.pdf).

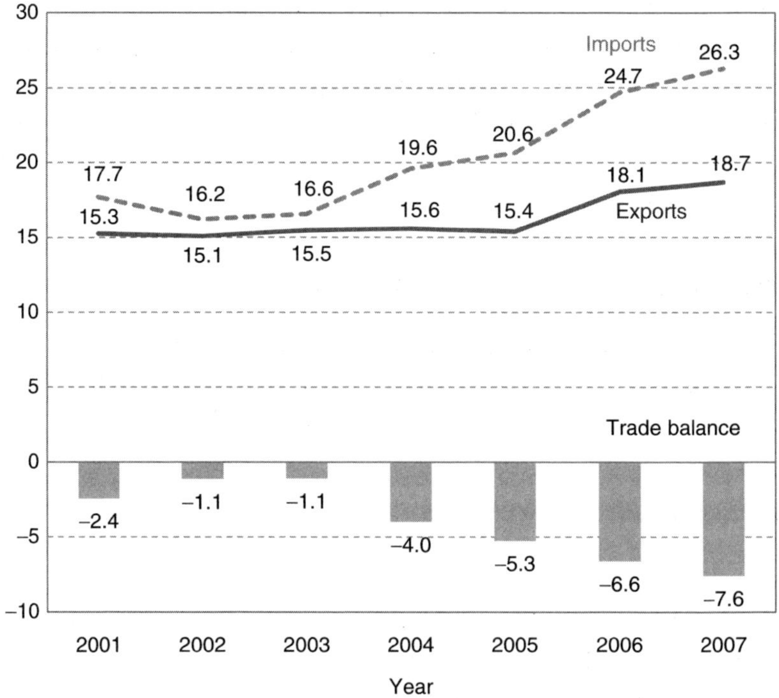

Fig. 1: Singapore's merchandise exports, import and trade balance with the USA (in $ billion).

Source: International Monetary Fund.

Table 2: Singapore's export market shares in percentage.

Rank in 2008	Export destination	2001	2008
1	Malaysia	17.3	12.1
2	Indonesia	10.6	10.5
3	Hong Kong	8.9	10.3
4	China	4.4	9.2
5	The United States	15.4	7.1
6	Japan	7.7	4.9
7	Australia	2.6	4.1
8	Thailand	4.4	3.9
9	South Korea	3.8	3.6
	Rest of the world	24.9	34.3

Source: International Enterprise Singapore.

has slipped from being second-top export destination in 2001 to the fifth in 2008. Similarly, the share of exports for major trading partners such as Malaysia, Japan, and Thailand has also decreased while that of China, Hong Kong, and the rest of the world has risen. This may suggest that though traditional markets remain important as export destinations, Singapore is also expanding its trade into other markets.

Pharmaceuticals exports has emerged as a major export item following the USSFTA and has grown tremendously over the last few years, from $126.3 million (US$91.8 million) in 2004 to $2.6 billion (US$1.9 billion) in 2008, an increase of nearly 2,000% as shown in Fig. 2. It ranked third among Singapore's exports to the USA in

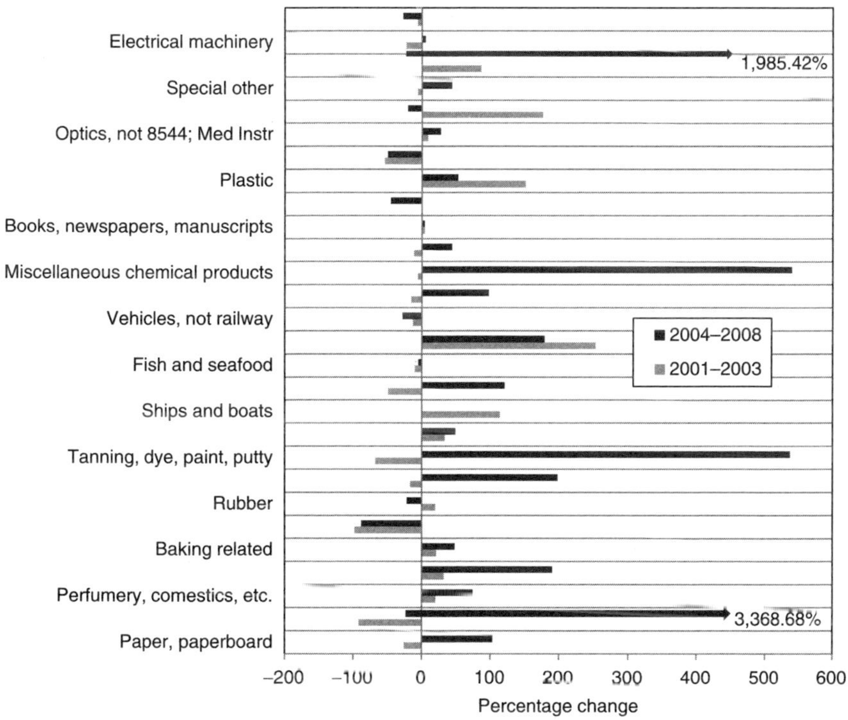

Fig. 2: Growth in Singapore's exports by two-digit harmonised system sectors.
Source: UN Comtrade.

2008. Together with machinery and electrical machinery, they account for more than half of total exports from Singapore. It must be noted that most are exports from MNCs which include those from the USA. To what extend the reduction in US tariffs under the FTA has contributed to the jump in pharmaceutical exports is unclear as it has been pointed out that such products already enter US duty-free even prior to the FTA. But the USSFTA has led to policy reforms such as legislative changes that include the strengthening of the Intellectual Property Rights (IPR) regime. As a result, a number of US companies have relocated to Singapore, such as Pfizer's $479 million multi-purpose active pharmaceutical ingredient manufacturing facility.[2]

Concurrently, Singapore has also been pushing to develop itself into a regional centre for multinational pharmaceutical companies, both for manufacturing and for research and development, which include setting up of biomedical facilities aside from IPR reforms (Nanto, 2008). This has shown results as the city-state is increasingly becoming a base for both regional and global pharmaceutical production for a growing number of multinational companies. Much of the production is for export, particularly to the USA and Europe. Singapore is also a major importer of pharmaceuticals from other Asian countries for re-export. Before the FTA, a sizable proportion of Singapore's pharmaceutical exports were transshipments from other countries. Though such re-exports continue to increase, they are now far-exceeded by exports of domestic production as shown in Fig. 3.

The country's manufacturers and exporters have gained a competitive edge through tariff savings and from a harmonisation of customs rules and procedures. Under the USSFTA, US importers saved 3% on import duties previously imposed on electronic packaging. This benefited small- and medium-sized enterprises (SMEs).

---

[2] How Singapore benefited from the FTA with the USA (http://www.mfa.gov.sg/seoul/pdf/USSFTA_final.pdf).

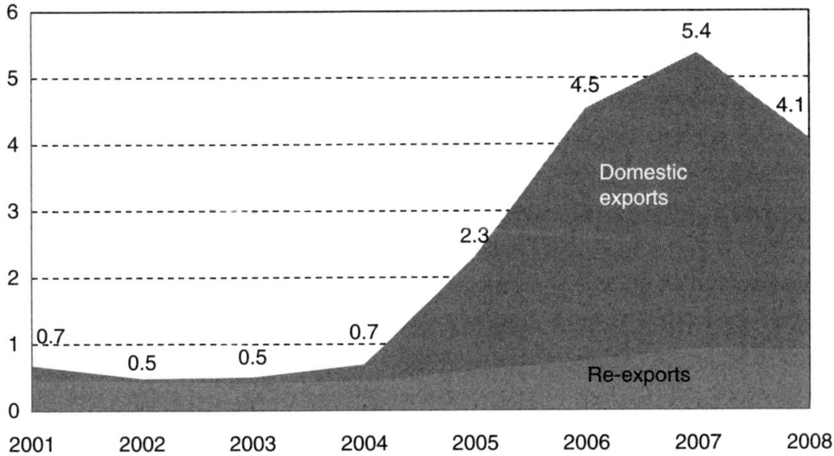

Fig. 3: Singapore's exports of pharmaceutical products (in $ billion).

Source: International Enterprise Singapore.

Singapore's imports from the USA

Though Singapore has increased its imports from the USA substantially, the US share of total imports has declined from 16.4% in 2001 to 11.9% in 2008 as summarised in Table 3. The share of imports from Malaysia and Japan has also fallen during this period, while that of China, Taiwan, South Korea, and Saudi Arabia has risen, suggesting that Singapore is looking beyond its traditional import sources towards China and Taiwan and other countries outside the region. While Malaysia and the USA remain the top two major sources of imports, China has overtaken Japan. By 2008, China was ranked third among Singapore's import markets.

Singapore's imports from the USA have been showing a sharp upward trend since 2003, and though exports have been increasing, the balance of trade has widened significantly in favour of the USA. The main imports from the USA are machinery, electrical machinery, aircraft and spacecraft, and mineral fuel and oil.

Table 3: Singapore's import market shares in percentage.

Rank in 2008	Export destination	2001	2008
1	Malaysia	17.3	11.9
2	United States	16.4	11.7
3	China	6.2	10.6
4	Japan	13.9	8.1
5	Taiwan	4.3	5.1
6	Indonesia	7.1	5.5
7	South Korea	3.3	5.6
8	Saudi Arabia	3.6	4.6
9	Thailand	4.4	3.5
	Rest of the world	23.4	33.3

Source: International Enterprise Singapore.

Trade in Services

US businesses believe that the greatest effect from the USSFTA is the potential of increased access to Singapore's market in services, which is also a key sector in Singapore's economy. Unlike merchandise trade, the financial sector was not as open. Thus, it was understood during the negotiations of the agreement that the USA would lower its tariffs and other restrictions on merchandise trade in exchange for Singapore liberalising access to its services sector, with financial services being the key component (Koh, 2004).

Singapore has traditionally run a deficit in its overall balance of trade in services with the USA, but this deficit shrank from $4 billion in 2001 to $2.1 billion in 2005 before increasing in the subsequent years, and by 2008 it reached slightly below the level it was in 2001, as shown in Fig. 4. Among the four components of the services trade, travel and transportation have largely remained in the surplus though the size varies over the years. Transportation accounts for most of it, especially shipping, and the rest are passenger fares and travel. Government and military transactions came out of the red in 2006 and posted a surplus of $170 million and increased to $610 million in 2008. In royalties and license fees, the deficit deepened over the years from $2.5 billion in 2001 to $3.1 billion in 2008. The

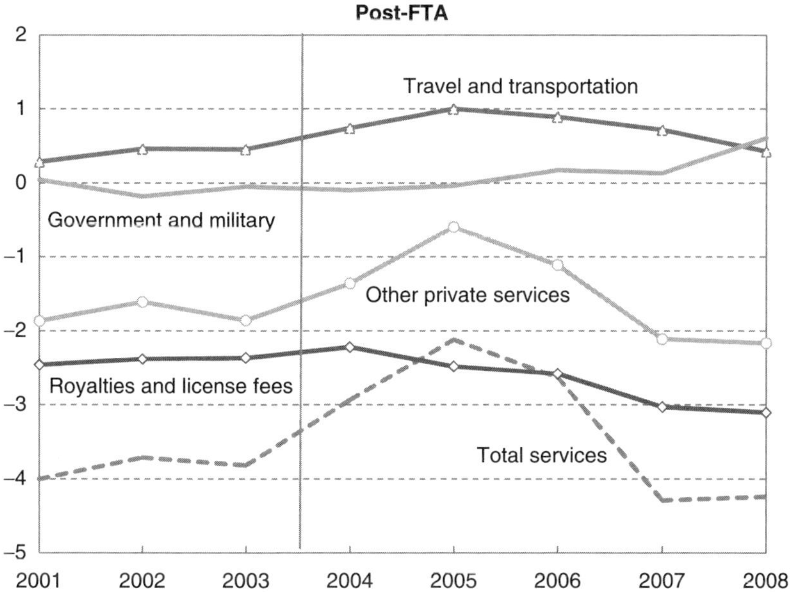

Fig. 4: Singapore's balance of trade with USA in services and its components (in $ billion).

Source: US Bureau of Economic Analysis.

deterioration could be partly the result of increased fee for intellectual property attributed to the strengthened IP protection in Singapore resulting from the FTA (Nanto, 2008).

With regard to financial services, the USSFTA has speeded up the banking liberalisation programme that was started in 1990s. Under the USSFTA, the Singapore government lifted the ban on new licences for full-service and wholesale US banks. US banks with subsidiaries in Singapore were given full access to Singapore's domestic banking market. The increased competition has spurred the existing Singapore banks to improve their capabilities and service standards and expand into new activities and new international markets.[3] But a US government report stated that despite

[3] How Singapore benefited from the FTA with the USA (http://www.mfa.gov.sg/seoul/pdf/USSFTA_final.pdf).

liberalisation, USA and other foreign banks in the domestic retail banking sector still face barriers such as constraints on customer service locations or access to the local ATM (automated teller machines) network. Holders of credit cards issued locally by foreign banks or other financial institutions cannot access their accounts through the local ATM networks. They are also unable to access their accounts for cash withdrawals, transfers, or bill payments at ATMs operated by banks other than those operated by their own bank or at foreign banks' shared ATM network. Nevertheless, full-service foreign banks have made significant inroads in other retail banking areas, such as credit cards and personal and housing loans.[4]

In legal services, Singapore has in the past few years relaxed its rules on foreigners practicing law in the republic to address a perceived shortage of practicing lawyers, although restrictions remain in certain areas including criminal law, family law, and domestic litigation. USA and other foreign lawyers have been allowed to represent parties in arbitration in Singapore without the need for a Singapore attorney to be present. US law firms can provide legal services with respect to Singapore law provided it is through a joint venture or formal alliance with a Singapore law firm. Law degrees from Harvard, Columbia, University of Michigan, and New York University are now recognised for admission to the Singapore bar. This has given Singaporean students a wider choice of universities to study law, as well as allowed Singapore-based firms to recruit talent from a broader catchment.

At the same time, Singapore companies now have guaranteed access to the US market in several service sectors, such as telecommunications. The USSFTA has also eased travel by Singapore's investors and employees of Singapore's companies to the USA and to stay in the USA for extended periods.[5]

---

[4] USTR (2009). National Trade Estimate Report on Foreign Trade Barriers (http://www.ustr.gov/sites/default/files/uploads/reports/2009/NTE/asset_upload_file107_15504.pdf).

[5] How Singapore benefited from the FTA with the USA (http://www.mfa.gov.sg/seoul/pdf/USSFTA_final.pdf).

Table 4: US and Singapore bilateral investment (in $ million).

Year	Singapore investment in the USA	US investment in Singapore
2001	−1,451	5,593
2002	−485	530
2003	1,097	5,447
2004	348	8,064
2005	798	3,207
2006	2,216	8,036
2007	5,677	13,406
2008	1,437	10,731
2009	39	7,458

Source: US Bureau of Economic Analysis.

Investment

Companies from both countries have also taken the opportunity created by market access and reduction in tariffs coupled with a conducive business environment to invest in each other's shores. US investment following the USSFTA grew yearly from $5.4 billion in 2003 to $13.4 billion in 2007 before slowing down in the subsequent two years which could be attributed to the economic downturn as summarised in Table 4. Nonetheless, the country remains a major investor and was the largest investor in Singapore in 2008.

Major companies that have invested in Singapore include US-based biotech giant Genentech, now a wholly owned subsidiary of Swiss company Roche.[6] It has opened a new complex in Singapore in the Tuas Biomedical Park that houses a $290 million biologics manufacturing facility to produce drug substance for Avastin, as well as invested in a new facility to produce drugs such as Lucentis, which is used to treat a form of blindness. This gives an added boost to Singapore's biomedical and pharmaceutical sector. In 2004,

[6] "Roche opens first Asia-Pacific biologics manufacturing site," 3 November 2009, Singapore Economic Development Board website (http://www.sedb.com/edb/sg/en_uk/index/news/articles/roche_opens_first.html).

Motorola established its 3G research and development centre in Singapore. This facility is the company's first in the world to have a full value-chain of activities in a single location on the 3G front churning out 3G phones for markets in South-East Asia, Australia, New Zealand, Taiwan, Europe, and the USA.[7] Another example is Reed HyCalog's (a division of Grant Prideco, a leading oilfield equipment manufacturer) $22 million investment in its manufacturing operations. This move was encouraged by the tariff savings from the immediate elimination of 5% duty for drill bits under the USSFTA (coupled with lower production costs in Singapore). While some of these investments were motivated by the US market, others came to take advantage of the FTA's access to other countries. A US company based in Utah, Huntsman, has invested US$35 million in Singapore on its first manufacturing facility to produce polyetheramine (used in fuel and lubricant additives, herbicides, and pesticides) aimed at the Asia-Pacific, including Australia.

Singaporean companies have also taken advantage of the opportunities presented by the USSFTA to invest in the USA. The FTA also opened new sectors in the US economy, such as government procurement. Investment from Singapore rose in the first few years from $348 million in 2004 to $5.6 billion in 2007 before sliding back sharply in subsequent years. One of the Singapore companies which benefited is Bodynits International, a contract manufacturer for active fitness apparel, whose customers include major global brands such as Adidas, Fila, Nike, and Puma. The FTA allows the companies' buyers to gain in tariff savings under the tariff preferential scheme. As a result, Bodynits International's products have become more price-competitive as compared with those manufactured by companies from other countries, and this has boosted its exports. Without the scheme, Bodynits International's synthetic fabrics garments would be subject to a duty of up to 33%.[8] Other companies

---

[7] How Singapore benefited from the FTA with the USA (http://www.mfa.gov.sg/seoul/pdf/USSFTA_final.pdf).

[8] *Ibid.*

that managed to gain businesses from the USA include: ST Engineering which won a contract worth US$200 million ($275 million) to supply rugged laptop computers to the US Army; Koda, a furniture manufacturer, won a contract to supply Pottery Barn with $22 million worth of furniture; Aztech Systems, a manufacturer of multimedia products and computer peripherals, clinched orders worth US$20 million ($27.5 million) for its ADSL products; WinEdge & Wireless won a contract to supply communication chips for a new product by US toy manufacturer, Hasbro. Whether big or small, companies such as Singapore Airlines, NOL/APL, ST Electronics, Keppel, SembCorp, Creative, Asia Pacific Breweries, Osim, Eu Yan Sang, and Tee Yih Jia have increased their presence in the USA.[9]

Intellectual Property Rights

The non-economic effects brought about by the USSFTA are in the area of policy reforms such that Singapore now has one of the strongest IPR regimes in the region. In July 2004, amendments were made to the Trademarks Act, the Patents Act, the Layout Designs of Integrated Circuits Act, Registered Designs Act; a new Plant Varieties Protection Act and a new Manufacture of Optical Discs Act came into effect. This was followed in 2005 by an amended Copyright Act and Broadcasting Act. Also included was implementation or ratification of various international conventions or treaties dealing with IPRs (Nanto, 2008). As a result, a number of US companies have relocated or made new investments to Singapore. They are Microsoft's Innovation Centre, Lucas Film Animation's studio and production house, and a Pfizer manufacturing plant. Others, which were also mentioned above, such as Motorola and Genentech, also made new investments in operations in Singapore.

[9] "USSFTA: The year in review," 29 January 2005. International Enterprise Singapore website (http://tinyurl.com/y4eukrv).

CONCLUSION

While much hope is placed on FTAs as the key driver of economic growth, this review shows that although the USSFTA has stimulated trade and investment, the trend somewhat suggests that sustained growth is uncertain. In terms of merchandise trade, Singapore's exports to the USA have been falling behind USA's exports to the city-state in the five years since the agreement was enforced. Singapore's trade deficit jumped from $1.1 billion to a whopping $12.7 billion in 2008, suggesting that trade growth is not as forthcoming in spite of the lowering of tariffs in the USA. However, a closer look at the performance of the various sectors shows that certain sectors performed better than others. Pharmaceutical exports, in particular, have been doing very well, posting a nearly 2,000% increase between 2004 and 2008. But one needs to bear in mind that MNCs, some of whom are American, have a significant presence in Singapore. Of the total exports, increasingly more and more of Singapore's exports come from domestic sources rather than from other countries for re-export from Singapore. This may reflect the growing role played by the development of the biomedical sector in part contributed by the strengthening of IPR protection in the wake of the USSFTA.

The SME communities especially those involved in electronics manufacturing have also benefited by the elimination of the 3% on import duties in the USA, making their products more competitive.

While the tightening of IPR provisions may be attractive to draw foreign companies seeking greater protection for their products, the flip side is that it can exert a higher toll in the form of increased fee for intellectual property resulting from the FTA. This is reflected in the deepening of the deficit in Singapore's royalties and license fees component of its services trade between 2001 and 2008.

Can those countries either planning to enter into or already engaged in an FTA with a major economy like the US glean any lessons from the experience of Singapore? While each country's circumstances and structures vary and, therefore, cognisance should be given to such differences, Singapore's experience thus far with the USSFTA can be instructive for countries that have already entered into or plan to engage in talks with the USA or EU, another party which has been actively engaging bilateral talks with countries in the region and like the USA, it adopts the WTO-plus type of agreements.

One of the main objectives of FTAs is to boost bilateral trade. As shown in this review, though tariff levels in partner country may come down, it does not necessarily translate into substantial growth in export figures, as in the case of Singapore in its FTA with the USA. Countries also must be prepared for an influx in imports and be vigilant as to how this may have impact on local producers. As the Singapore experience shows even though almost all US products enjoy relatively free-tariff in Singapore before the USSFTA and exports were therefore expected to increase substantially, nevertheless, imports from the USA into Singapore increased significantly post-FTA. As such, for other countries which have high tariff rates, the impact could be quite drastic in terms of rise in imports if tariffs are eliminated.

With regard to foreign direct investment, which is a key objective of any FTAs, the FTA has stimulated two-way investments as companies take advantage of the reduction in business costs due to the elimination of duties and the strengthened IP regime; however, there is no clear trend as the growth of US investment into Singapore varies over the years under review and vice versa.

REFERENCES

Asian Development Bank FTA Database (http://www.aric.adb.org/index.php).

Desker, B. (2004). In defense of FTAs: From purity to pragmatism in East Asia. *The Pacific Review*, 17(1), 3–26.

Dent, C. M. (2006). *New Free Trade Agreements in the Asia-Pacific*. London: Palgrave Macmillan.

Feinberg, R. (2006). US Trade Arrangements in the Asia-Pacific. In *Bilateral Trade Agreements in the Asia-Pacific*, V. Aggarwal and S. Urata (eds.). New York and London: Routledge.

Kawai, M. (2007). *Evolving Economic Architecture in East Asia,* ADBI Working Paper Series, No. 84, December 2007, Asian Development Bank Institute, Tokyo.

Koh, T. and Chang, L. L. (eds.) (2004). *The United States-Singapore Free Trade Agreement: Highlights and Insights,* Institute of Policy Studies. Singapore: Singapore and World Scientific Publishing.

Koh, T. (2004). The USSFTA: A Personal Perspective. In T. Koh and L. L. Chang (eds.). *The United States Singapore Free Trade Agreement: Highlights and Insights,* Institute of Policy Studies. Singapore: Singapore and World Scientific Publishing.

Lee, Seungjoo (2006). Singapore Trade Bilateralism. In *Bilateral Trade Agreements in the Asia-Pacific,* V. Aggarwal and S. Urata (eds.). New York and London: Routledge.

Low, L. (2006). *The Political Economy of a City-State Revisited.* Singapore: Marshall Cavendish.

Nanto, D. (2008). The US-Singapore free trade agreement: Effects after three years. Congressional Research Service, 7 January 2008.

Chapter 9
STATE CAPITALISM IN SINGAPORE

SNG Hui Ying

State-owned enterprises (SOEs) have played critical roles in Singapore's economic development. During the early phase of Singapore's industrialisation process, these SOEs played the role of state entrepreneurs. They were also builders of infrastructure and providers of essential services. Since then, SOEs have proliferated and expanded in scope and involvement in the economy. Their dominant position in the economy raised concerns, particularly in the 1980s and 1990s, that the SOEs were competing unfairly against domestic private entrepreneurs and were stifling the growth of domestic private entrepreneurship. The government has responded to these concerns by corporatising, public listing, and divesting many of the SOEs. This chapter provides an overview of state capitalism in Singapore — its roles, its evolution, its performance, and why SOEs in Singapore have avoided the many pitfalls commonly associated with SOEs elsewhere.

INTRODUCTION

In 1960, Singapore government set up the Housing and Development Board (HDB). This was followed by the National Iron and Steel Mills Ltd (NISM)[1] in 1961, the Public Utilities Board

[1] NISM was later renamed Natsteel.

(PUB) in the 1963, the Jurong Shipyard[2] in 1963, the Port of Singapore Authority (PSA) in 1964, the Chartered Industries of Singapore (CIS)[3] in 1967, the Far East Shipbuilding Industries in 1967, the Development Bank of Singapore (DBS) in 1968, the Intraco in 1968, the Jurong Town Corporation (JTC) in 1968, the Sembawang Shipyard in 1968, the Singapore Shipbuilding & Engineering (SSE)[4] in 1968, the Singapore Electronic & Engineering Pte Ltd (SEEL)[5] in 1969, the Jurong Bird Park in 1970, the Singapore Technologies Automotive in 1971, the Singapore Automotive Engineering (SAE)[6] in 1971, the Post Office Savings Bank (POSB) in 1972, the Telecommunication Authority of Singapore (TAS) in 1974, the Singapore Technologies Aerospace in 1975, the URA Property Management Division[7] in 1979, the Singapore Test Services in 1980, the National Computer Board (NCB) in 1981, the SAE Inspection Centre[8] in 1982, the Singapore Commuters[9] in 1983, the Mass Rapid Transit Corporation (MRTC)[10] in 1984, and the list goes on. Established with the primary objectives of catalysing the industrialisation process and providing basic economic services, state capitalism has become an important driving force in the economic development of Singapore.

---

[2] Jurong Shipyard Ltd was established in 1963 as a joint venture between the Government of Singapore and Ishikawajima Harima Heavy Industries Co Ltd (IHI) of Japan. It is now a wholly owned subsidiary of Sembcorp Marine.

[3] CIS was merged with ST Automotive in 2000 to form ST Kinetics.

[4] SSE is now known as ST Marine.

[5] SEEL is now known as ST Electronics.

[6] SAE was later renamed Singapore Technologies Automotive (ST Auto). ST Auto was merged with CIS in 2000 to form ST Kinetics.

[7] URA Property Management Division was corporatised to become Pidemco Land in 1989. Pidemco Land was later merged with main-board listed DBS Land to form CapitaLand in 2000.

[8] SAE Inspection Centre is now known as STA Inspection.

[9] Singapore Commuters was merged with Singapore Airport Services and Singapore Bus Service Taxi to form CityCab in April 1995.

[10] MRTC was later renamed SMRT Corporation.

State-owned enterprises (SOEs) in Singapore have chiefly been embodied in statutory boards (SBs) and in government-linked companies (GLCs). The SBs operate outside the government budget and with greater autonomy than government departments, but they are still accountable to their respective ministries which provide policy guidelines on major matters. Many SBs were later corporatised and publicly listed and thus transformed into GLCs. GLCs, on the other hand, are enterprises incorporated under the Companies Act, just like any private-sector company. GLCs may be wholly owned or are joint ventures with the private sector. Singapore government manages the majority of its investment in GLCs via Temasek Holdings, a limited holding company.

SBs and GLCs have played critical roles in Singapore's economic development. During the early phase of Singapore's industrialisation process, these SOEs played the role of state entrepreneurs. They were also builders of infrastructure and providers of banking, transportation, and telecommunication services. Since the 1960s, SOEs have proliferated and expanded in scope and involvement in the economy. A 1987 report by the Public Sector Divestment Committee put the total number of GLCs, including those with minority government ownership, at about 500 (Bercuson, 1995). Their dominant position in the economy raised concerns, particularly in the 1980s and 1990s, that the GLCs were unfairly competing against domestic private entrepreneurs and were stifling the growth of domestic private entrepreneurship. The government has responded to these concerns by corporatising, public-listing, and divesting many of the SBs and GLCs.

This chapter aims to provide an overview of state capitalism in Singapore — its roles, its evolution, its performance, and why have SOEs in Singapore avoided the many pitfalls commonly associated with SOEs elsewhere. The chapter ends with a discussion on the new wave of state capitalism — Sovereign Wealth Funds.

THE BEGINNING OF STATE CAPITALISM IN SINGAPORE

At the time of independence in 1965, Singapore was besieged by a multitude of economic problems which include a high rate of unemployment, severe housing shortage, and huge deficiency in national savings. The secession of Singapore from the Federation of Malaysia spelled the loss of the access to the Malaysian hinterland market and together with it, the end of the import-substitution policies. To further compound the problem of high unemployment, Britain announced in January 1968 her decision to withdraw all of Britain's 35,000 troops stationed in Singapore by end 1971. At that time, the British military base contributed a fifth of Singapore's GDP. It was Singapore's largest industry and provided direct employment to 10% of the labour force (Omar, 2007).

The urgent need to create large-scale employment opportunities formed the logical basis for Singapore to adopt industrialisation as her initial growth strategy in the early 1960s. As compared with trade and services sectors, labour-intensive manufacturing sector has the ability to absorb many more lowly-skilled and lowly educated workers.

However, during the British colonial rule, the British authorities had pursued a *laissez faire* economic policy within the general framework of a small open economy which had led to a flourishing trade and commerce sector but a relatively underdeveloped manufacturing sector. Although the Chinese entrepreneurs had successfully established their foothold in trade and commerce, banking and finance, insurance, real estate development, and construction, they were seldom involved in manufacturing industries (Tan, 1996). Thus, when the Singapore government planned to move away from a heavy dependence on trade and services towards a larger manufacturing sector, they found that the Chinese commercial entrepreneurs were not ready to become industrial entrepreneurs (Tan, 1996).

To circumvent the problem of the lack of domestic industrial entrepreneurs, the Singapore government turned to foreign entrepreneurship and state entrepreneurship to provide the backbone of Singapore's industrialisation strategy. On the one hand, Singapore warmly reached out to foreign multinational companies (MNCs), offering them fiscal incentives and promises of political stability, industrial peace, and subsequently, free trade. These MNCs brought along with them capital, technological know-how, managerial expertise, and export markets. In 1965, there were only 47 wholly owned foreign firms in the manufacturing sector in Singapore. By 1989, this increased to 595, contributing to 63% of the total value added of the manufacturing sector (Lim, 1991). In 2008, foreign firms' investment commitment in manufacturing and services sectors was S$16.18 billion, which was 90% of total investment commitment.

On the other hand, the Singapore government proactively established SBs and GLCs in key sectors of the economy where private enterprise was perceived to be lacking, such as banking and finance, public utilities, transport and logistics, shipbuilding, telecommunication services, broadcasting services, and port services. The setting up of SBs and GLCs was often justified on the grounds that these industries were of strategic importance to Singapore, but local private investment was not forthcoming.

In addition, some of the SBs and the GLCs, such as the HDB[11] and CIS,[12] were set up with the objective of fulfilling certain social needs and security needs. Some of the SOEs were products of institutional evolution, such as Singapore Airlines (SIA), which was formed after the split of a national airlines company between Singapore and Malaysia, and Sembawang Shipyard and Keppel Shipyard, which were set up to run the former British naval docks and repair facilities on a commercial basis (Ow, 1986). The setting up of the GLCs has also helped Singapore to build up her comparative advantages in certain industries. For example, Keppel Shipyard, Sembawang Shipyard, and Jurong Shipyard have helped spur the development of Singapore as a major shipbuilding and ship repair centre.

---

[11] HDB is the planner and developer of public housing in Singapore.

[12] CIS is a manufacturer of ammunition and small arms. Singapore's defence industries were established in the late 1960s with the objective of reducing the country's reliance on foreign countries to supply weapons and war vessels, and to provide indigenous support to Singapore's armed force.

TEMASEK HOLDINGS — THE HOLDING COMPANY

A discussion on GLCs in Singapore inevitably will involve Temasek Holdings. Temasek Holdings is a limited holding company established by the Singapore government in 1974 to manage its investment in the GLCs. At that time, 35 companies were transferred to Temasek Holdings.[13] In the 1990s, SBs such as SingTel, SingPower, and PSA were corporatised and transferred to Temasek. By March 2010, Temasek has grown to a global firm that manages a diversified portfolio of S$186 billion. The list of major Singaporean GLCs held by Temasek is given in Table 1.

Temasek Holdings has repeatedly pointed out that the company is "guided by an independent board and it operates *autonomously* on commercial principles to maximise long-terms returns" (Temasek Holdings, 2009). In other words, there is no government interference. In view of the general suspicion of the objectives of Sovereign Wealth Funds on the global front and sporadic criticisms of unfair advantages enjoyed by the GLCs on the domestic front, Temasek needs to be very cautious in managing the public perception of its role and its autonomy.

Over the years, Temasek Holdings has overseen the corporatisation, public-listing, merger and acquisition, divestment, and regionalisation/globalisation of the GLCs. Temasek Holdings has also steadily increased its investment in foreign corporations. In 2010, 32% of its S$186 billion portfolio is invested in Singapore. This is significantly lower than the 52% investment in Singapore in 2004 and is in part due to Temasek's active investment in foreign corporations, especially financial institutions, in the recent years. For example, Temasek Holdings invested in Bank of China in 2005,

[13] Around the same time, Sheng-Li Holdings (now Singapore Technologies) were set up as the holding company of the defence-related GLCs. Another holding company that was set up was MND Holdings (owned by the Ministry of National Development), but MND Holdings was subsequently taken over by the Ministry of Finance and the bulk of its GLCs was transferred to Temasek Holdings (Ramírez and Tan, 2003).

Table 1: Major GLCs held by Temasek Holdings.

Company	Shareholding (%) as of 31 March 2010
Financial services	
DBS Group Holdings*	28
Telecommunications, media and technology	
Mediacorp	100
Singapore Technologies Telemedia	100
Singapore Telecommunications*	54
STATS ChipPAC*	84
Transport and industrial	
Neptune Orient Lines*	66
PSA International	100
Singapore Airlines*	54
SMRT Corporation*	54
Singapore Airport Terminal Services*	44
Keppel Corporation*	21
Sembcorp Industries*	49
Singapore Technologies Engineering*	50
Real estates	
CapitaLand*	39
Mapletree Investments	100
Energy and resources	
Singapore Power	100
Consumer and life sciences	
Wildlife Reserves Singapore	88
Olam International*	14
Fraser and Neave	15

Source: Temasek Report, 2010.
Note: * Listed on Singapore Exchange.

China Construction Bank in 2005, NIB Bank in 2005, and Standard Chartered in 2006.[14]

[14] Temasek's foray into investment in global financial institutions saw it acquiring stakes in Barclays and Merrill Lynch in 2007, during the early phase of the global financial crisis. It also ended up with a Bank of America (BOA) stake when BOA bought Merrill Lynch. In 2009, Temasek announced that it was refocusing on emerging markets and sold off its entire stake in BOA and Barclays at a substantial loss.

CRITICISMS OF STATE CAPITALISM

Very often, SOEs conjure up images of inefficient and bloated organisations that are a drain on the government's fiscal budget. Alternatively, SOEs are sometimes perceived as government-back bullies that encroach on the turf of domestics small-medium enterprises (SMEs). The first criticism is related to the tendency of SOEs to be inefficient, while the second criticism is associated with unfair or excessive competition posed by SOEs on private enterprises.

Inefficiency of SOEs

There are several arguments that explain the lacklustre performance of SOEs as compared with private-owned enterprises (POEs), and very often these arguments are related to the differing objectives of the two types of enterprises.

While the primary objective of POEs is usually profit maximisation, the objectives of SOEs could be influenced by the political objectives of politicians and bureaucrats. As students of Economics have learned from their Econ 101, the objective of profit maximisation brings about several desirable outcomes in a competitive market, such as efficiency in the allocation of resources (i.e., allocative efficiency) and efficiency in the utilisation of resources and choice of production processes (i.e., productive efficiency). In the scenario where SOEs are shielded from competition through artificial barriers to entry, the losses from efficiencies and social welfare are even greater.

As the operations of SOEs are more influenced by budgetary allocation than profit generation, SOEs tend to be less sensitive to market conditions. Market discipline may also be lacking as governments tend to bail out poorly run SOEs, often due to concerns over potential job losses or that the SOEs are providers of some key services. The lack of market discipline also leads to SOEs being less concerned about efficiency improvement and better resource utilisation. In addition, the hiring of resources by the SOEs may be politically motivated rather than commercially motivated. Boycko *et al.* (1996) argue that as one key objective of politicians is employment, politicians cause SOEs to employ excess workers. In the event government needs to subsidise loss-making SOEs or to bail out failing SOEs, strain would be placed on the fiscal budget of the government.

Moreover, the corporate culture of SOEs is often similar to that of the public sector where risk-taking behaviours are commonly frowned upon and not adequately rewarded, resulting in SOEs that tend to be more bureaucratic and less innovative. SOEs may also be prone to corruption as decisions may be made for political reasons or for the personal gain of the decision makers, such as hiring of politically connected persons or awarding of lucrative contracts to political cronies.

It was largely due to these considerations that privatisation of SOEs gained worldwide momentum in the 1980s, with United Kingdom's then Prime Minister Margaret Thatcher and the United States' President Ronald Reagan being staunch advocates of privatisation of SOEs.

However, as pointed out by Vining and Boardman (1992), in sectors where there are massive economies of scale and scope, high entry barriers, or externalities, public ownership may be preferred to private ownership.

Competition Between SOEs and POEs

The second criticism is that SOEs crowd out private-sector investment and may hinder the development of local enterprises. This is especially the case when SOEs compete with local enterprises in sectors traditionally dominated by local enterprises or in sectors where natural monopoly does not exist. For that matter, the dominance of SOEs in Singapore has frequently been cited as the reason for the dearth of local entrepreneurship.

There are also perceived unfair advantages enjoyed by the SOEs when they compete in the same industry as the local enterprises — SOEs, having the backing of the government, may be able to obtain credits cheaply or be given lucrative government contracts.

EMPIRICAL STUDIES ON SOEs

There has been a voluminous literature on the performances of SOEs vs. POEs, or performances of SOEs before and after privatisation. Empirical studies have often confirmed the lacklustre performance of the public enterprises. Survey of studies done by Donahue (1989) shows the cost of public provision of municipal services is significantly higher than that of the private provision in the United States. Survey of studies done by Mueller (1989) and Vining and Boardman (1992) also show that in most studies of public and private firms around the world, private firms are found to be more efficient. Studies by Megginson *et al.* (1994), Lopez de Silanes (1997), DeWenter and Malatesta (2001), and D'Souza *et al.* (2001) all indicate that public companies (or pre-privatised SOEs) are less profitable than privately owned companies (or post-privatised SOEs). However, Bozec *et al.* (2002) present empirical evidence that the GLCs, if their main goal is to maximise profit, can perform as well as the private enterprises.

Amid the sea of negative reports on SOEs, Singapore's GLCs clearly stand out as a clear example to the contrary. Empirical studies on Singapore often show SOEs outperforming POEs in Singapore.

Profitability and Efficiency

The study by Ang and Ding (2006) compares the financial and market performance of GLCs and non-GLCs over an 11-year-period from 1990 to 2000. Using return on equity and return on assets, they find that the profitability of GLCs outperformed non-GLCs. Feng *et al.* (2004) study 30 Singapore's GLCs for the period 1964–1998 and point out that there was no evidence that the GLCs were less profitable than a selected group of non-GLCs that match by size and industry. These findings concur with those of Singh and

Ang (1998) and Sabhlok (2001) that Singapore's GLCs are able to achieve at least similar levels of profitability and are as efficient as non-GLCs.

Market Valuation

Ramírez and Tan (2003) compare the Tobin's q[15] of GLCs and non-GLCs and find evidence that the capital markets value GLCs more highly than non-GLCs. The positive and significant relation between the government link and q is robust to the inclusion of other variables, such as industry effects, size, monopoly power, profitability, and bankruptcy risk, which might affect the firm value and q. After taking these variables into consideration, the authors find that being a GLC is rewarded in the financial market with a premium of about 20%.

Ang and Ding (2006) have similar findings. The authors also compute the Tobin's q to determine the degree to which government involvement affects the firm value. They find that GLCs on average exhibit higher valuation than those of the non-GLCs, even after controlling for firm specific factors such as profitability, leverage, firm size, industry effect, and foreign ownership.

Ease of Access to Credit

Ramírez and Tan (2003) empirically investigate the question of whether Singapore's GLCs benefit from special financial advantages. The authors postulate that if the GLCs enjoy cheaper funding (and thus do not compete on equal footing with POEs), they will have an easier time raising funds compared with the POEs. If this is the case, liquidity should be irrelevant, or at least less important, as a determinant of GLCs' investment spending. Ramírez and Tan (2003) compare the differences in the effects of various determinants of

[15] Tobin's q is the ratio between the firm's market value and the replacement value of the book equity.

investment spending by GLCs and POEs and find no difference in liquidity constraints between GLCs and non-GLCs. The authors therefore conclude that GLCs do not have easier access to credit.

WHY DOES STATE CAPITALISM WORK IN SINGAPORE?

In many ways, Singapore's GLCs have avoided the usual pitfalls associated with SOEs from many other countries. Their performance in terms of profitability and efficiency are as good as, if not better than, those of the non-GLCs in Singapore. Singapore's GLCs not only do not require subsidies from the government, they in fact contribute to the coffer of the government when they pay out dividends to the shareholders, which include the Singapore government. Unsuccessful GLCs, for example, Singapore Aquarama, General Leather and Saber Air, were liquidated instead of being bailed out (Ow, 1986). The workability of state capitalism in Singapore can be attributed to the government's philosophy of GLCs, which has been carefully thought through, explicitly spelt out and conscientiously adhered to. Essentially, it is to subject the GLCs to the rigour of competitive market such that the drive to improve on efficiency and profitability is integrated into the operations of the GLCs.

Singapore government's philosophy of GLCs was articulated in the 2002 Budget Speech (Ministry of Finance, 2002). It was stated that GLCs have to operate as commercial entities, with no interference from the government with the operations of the GLCs. Thc GLCs are to be supervised by their respective boards of directors, who are accountable to their shareholders, including the government. It was also stated that the government will not favour GLCs with special privileges or hidden subsidies; nor will it burden them with uneconomic "national service" responsibilities. The GLCs are expected to compete on a level playing field, and frequently in a global environment.

The government also indicated that for GLCs that perform activities that are strategic and crucial to Singapore, such as aviation and the electricity grid, the government would retain its majority or significant stakes. For other major businesses with global or regional potential, Temasek will grow them to the benefit of Singapore over the long term. As for those GLCs that are no longer relevant to the government's objectives, the government will divest or dilute its shareholdings in a controlled way. The government also expressed their clear preference to have GLCs, strategic or otherwise, to be publicly listed rather than to be wholly owned. Public-listing will help to improve the transparency and accountability of the GLCs.

While the incentive problems and objective issues associated with public ownership could diminish efficiency, the competitiveness of the market itself is also important in achieving efficiency. In this aspect, the Singapore government has been working to introduce market competition into sectors where the GLCs operate in. One example is the telecommunication sector where the urgency to liberalise the market was particularly telling. When SingTel was corporatised in 1992, it was granted a 15-year monopoly till March 2007 to provide public basic domestic and international telecommunication services. At that time, telecommunication was considered a natural monopoly, and the homogenous service provided by SingTel was considered as adequate. However, technological advancement and increasing sophistication of the telecommunication market challenged these two assumptions. It became increasingly obvious to the government that the telecommunication market can and should be liberalised. In 1996, the government announced that SingTel's monopoly would be shortened to March 2000, after which a duopoly of SingTel and Starhub would operate till April 2002, after which full liberalisation will kick in.[16] However, even before Starhub could enter the market, the Singapore government again accelerated the date for full liberalisation to 1 April 2000. The results of the full liberalisation were encouraging — variety of services increased, quality of service improved, and prices lowered.[17]

---

[16] The mobile phone market was liberalised earlier in 1997 with the entry of Mobile One.

[17] Based on survey carried out by Infocomm Development Authority (IDA). Details of survey result are available at http://www.ida.gov.sg.

EVOLUTION OF GLCs IN SINGAPORE

In the 1960s, SOEs were chiefly industrial entrepreneurs, builders of infrastructure, and providers of essential services. Since then, SOEs have proliferated and expanded in various sectors of the economy. Many of the SOEs have also grown into sizable conglomerates and highly regarded enterprises. Two significant developments took place since 1980s — the corporatisation, privatisation and divestment of the SOEs, and the regionalisation and globalisation of the SOEs.

Corporatisation, Privatisation, and Divestment

In the mid-1980s, there was an increasing concern among domestic private entrepreneurs over perceived unfair competition posed by the public enterprises which were progressively encroaching on their domain. There were also complains that the public enterprises were crowding-out domestic private entrepreneurship (Lim, 1991). Partly because of these criticisms, the Public Sector Divestment Committee was formed in 1986 to look into ways of divesting and/or privatising public enterprises. The primarily objectives were to let the market mechanism and private sector play a larger role in the economy and to provide Singaporeans more opportunities to acquire a stake in local corporations. The Committee recommended that as many GLCs as possible should be privatised and the shareholdings of the government in listed companies should be reduced.[18] Since 1980s, Temasek has gradually reduced its shareholdings in GLCs such as SingTel, SIA, NOL, SMRT, CapitaLand, and Keppel Corporation. Over the years, Temasek has also divested the entire stake of many smaller and non-strategic GLCs including CPG Corp, Intraco, SingTel Yellow Pages, Changi International Airport Services Pte Ltd (CIAS), Natsteel, Singapore Food

[18] See Tan (1990) for the list of companies that Divestment Committee recommended (1) to be publicly listed, (2) to reduce government holdings, and (3) to be completely privatised.

Industries (SFI), Singapore Computer Systems, SNP Corporation, Chartered Semiconductor Manufacturing and Fraser and Neave. The three power-generating companies, Power Senoko, Tuas Power, and Power Seraya, were also divested in 2008 and 2009.

The Public Sector Divestment Committee also recommended the eventual privatisation of profit-making SBs such as the TAS (Telecom), components of the Public Utilities Board (PUB), the Civil Aviation Authority (CAA), and the PSA (Tan, 1992). Among these, Singapore Telecom (SingTel) was the first SB to be privatised. SingTel was corporatised in 1992, and an initial 11% of its share capital was sold to the public in 1993. It remains Singapore's largest ever Initial Public Offering (IPO).

The wave of corporatisation and privatisation of SBs continued, albeit at a gradual pace. The Public Sector Divestment Committee recommended a policy of decentralised initiative, i.e., the enterprises themselves should get ready for privatisation and seize the opportunities when they arise.

PSA was corporatised in October 1997 and renamed PSA Corporation Ltd. PSA was restructured in 2003, with PSA International becoming the main holding company for the PSA Group of companies. PSA International is still wholly owned by Temasek Holdings.

JTC began its corporatisation exercise in 2000 and was renamed JTC Corporation. Its port and technical services group was corporatised in 2001 to form Jurong Port Pte Ltd and Jurong Consultants Pte Ltd respectively. In the same year, its subsidiary, Arcasia Land, merged with the international operations arm of JTC International to form Ascendas Pte Ltd.[19] JTC provides an interesting example where government fixed assets, in this case industrial properties, are being securitised and divested. In 2002, Ascendas listed Ascendas Real Estate Investment Trust, a business and industrial space REIT, on the Singapore Exchange. In 2008, JTC divested a selected portfolio of high-rise ready-built properties worth S$1.71 billion to

[19] Ascendas focuses on Science Parks, IT Parks, and Business Parks in Singapore. It also develops and manages business space in China, India, South Korea, Vietnam, Malaysia, and the Philippines.

Mapletree Investments Pte Ltd. The initial plan was for Mapletree Investments to set up and manage the properties as a REIT. However the uncertain market condition at that time unsettled the plan. The initial public offering of Mapletree Industrial Trust was eventually launched in October 2010.

Changi Airport Group was only corporatised in 2009, with CAAS being restructured into a regulatory body that focuses on the development of the air hub and aviation industry in Singapore, as well as the provision of air navigation services. There were reports that the Singapore government was planning to sell the Changi Airport Group to Temasek Holdings.

In 2002, the Entrepreneurship and Internationalisation Subcommittee of the Economic Review Committee, led by the then minister of State of Ministry of Trade and Industry and Ministry of Foreign Affairs, Mr Raymond Lim, made further recommendations on the role of government in business (Economic Review Committee, 2002). Essentially, the subcommittee recommended that the chief objective of GLCs should be to manage critical resources, to achieve public policy objectives, and to develop new growth engines. Similar to the 1986 Public Sector Divestment Committee, the subcommittee recommended non-strategic GLCs to be divested. In addition, the subcommittee also recommended GLCs to internationalise their core businesses.

Despite the rhetoric of privatisation and divestment, the presence of GLCs in Singapore is still dominant, and Temasek's shareholdings in many of the listed GLCs are still above 50%. However, it has to be recognised that the government has made significant progress in corporatising and/or public-listing many of the SBs and GLCs. Corporatisation and public-listing of the SOEs will subject these enterprises to greater competition and scrutiny, which will in turn reduce many of the incentive problems mentioned earlier. By emphasising that "the government will not favour GLCs with special privileges or hidden subsidies," the government also seeks to assure the business community that competition between the GLCs and the private enterprises is unbiased. After all, Temasek does function as a Sovereign Wealth Fund that seeks to maximise returns.

Thus, if the GLCs in Singapore generate favourable returns, there will be no compelling reasons for Temasek to sell off its stakes unless attractive prices are being offered.

Regionalisation and Globalisation

The second development of Singapore's GLCs is their active expansion into the regional and global markets. Since late 1980s, there were increasing concerns among Singapore's policy makers that the small size of Singapore would constrain the future growth of Singapore if Singapore continued to be just a production base. In addition, there were also concerns about Singapore's over-dependence on electronic exports and Singapore's over-dependence on foreign capital. The Singapore government thus aimed to develop Singapore's external economy so as to build up the "second wing" of the Singapore economy. The investment could take the form of direct investment, portfolio investment, or foreign assets. As part of Singapore's national strategy to develop an "external wing," GLCs and SBs were roped in to spearhead Singapore's regionalisation and globalisation efforts (Yeung, 2000). Many SBs and government-linked conglomerates such as PSA International, Natsteel, CapitaLand, Mapletree Investments, SingTel, ST Telemedia, NOL, DBS Bank, SIA, JTC Corporation, Keppel Corporation, Sembcorp Industries, and ST Engineering have all set up overseas subsidiaries and made acquisitions in foreign lands.

NEW FACE OF STATE CAPITALISM

The regionalisation and globalisation efforts of Singapore's GLCs coincide with the rise of sovereign wealth funds (SWFs). SWFs are state-owned investment funds that invest globally in assets such as stocks, bonds, property, precious metals, or other financial instruments. While SWFs are not new, with the first being established as early as 1953, the number of countries that set up SWFs have soared in the recent years and the size of funds at their disposal is huge. Assets under management of SWFs were estimated to be around

US$3.8 trillion in 2009[20] and are expected to increase steadily in the coming years (Maslakovic, 2010). The rise in importance of SWFs has also changed the popular interpretation of state capitalism. In the past, state capitalism is taken to be state control of the economy. In the recent years, state capitalism is often closely associated with SWFs — Lyons (2007) defines state capitalism as "the use of government controlled funds to acquire strategic stakes around the world."

As the fund size of the SWFs grows, there is increasing scrutiny on the impacts and motives of these funds. One concern is the possible political intents of these investments to secure control of strategically important industries and resources. Another concern is the lack of transparency of these funds. Both concerns have led to some countries objecting to the sale of stakes of companies in strategic sectors.

In fact, the regionalisation and globalisation plans of Singapore's GLCs have occasionally suffered setback due to the reluctance of some recipient countries to allow SOE to invest in sectors considered nationally strategic. In 1999–2000, SingTel was defeated in takeover attempts of Hong Kong Telecom in Hong Kong and Time dotcom Malaysia largely for this reason. In 2007, Indonesia's anti-monopoly watchdog sanctioned and fined Temasek Holdings for breaking local competition laws and ordered Temasek Holdings to sell off its stake in either of Indonesia's two largest mobile-phone companies — Telkomsel[21] and Indosat[22] — claiming its cross-ownership in both had enabled it to fix prices and monopolise the market.[23]

---

[20] Estimates of the total fund size of SWFs vary from study to study due to the varying definitions of SWFs and the limited disclosure and lack of transparency of many SWFs. Using a narrow definition of SWFs, Lyons (2007) estimates the size of the top 22 SWFs to be US$2.2 trillion in 2007.

[21] SingTel owned 35% stake in Telkomsel.

[22] ST Telemedia owned 41.94% stake in Indosat.

[23] Telkomsel and Indosat together account for 75% of Indonesia's 80 million mobile users.

In comparison with some of the SWFs from China and the Middle Eastern Countries, Singapore's SWFs are viewed more favourably by many recipient nations. In a study by Lyons (2007), Singapore's Government Investment Corporation (GIC) is ranked third while Temasek Holdings is ranked seventh in terms of asset size among 22 largest SWFs. While both GIC and Temasek Holdings are ranked above average in terms of level of transparency (Temasek Holdings being more transparent than GIC), their investment approach is considered as strategic rather than conventional (Temasek Holdings being more strategic than GIC). The overseas investments by GLCs held by Temasek Holdings, such as SingTel, Telemedia, DBS, NOL, and PSA, are mostly, if not all, in strategic sectors such as telecommunication, banking, shipping, and port operation. Temasek Holdings also invest directly in financial intermediaries, for example Bank of China, China Construction Bank, and Standard Chartered, and media and telecommunication conglomerate Shin Corp.

Going forward, it is inevitable that the issue of government ownership would occasionally hamper efforts of Singapore's GLCs in acquiring stakes in foreign firms, especially if these firms operate in the strategic sectors. The International Monetary Fund (IMF) and Organization for Economic Co-operation and Development (OECD) are working to define a code of conduct for SWFs' transparency and accountability, which would identify good practices in terms of reporting, disclosure, auditing, and management structure (Elson, 2008). Widespread adoption and recognition of the code of conduct would be helpful to those Singapore's GLCs that are investing overseas.

REFERENCES

Ang, J. S. and D. K. Ding (2006). Government ownership and the performance of government-linked companies: The case of Singapore. *Journal of Multinational Financial Management*, 16(1), 64–88.

Bercuson, K. (1995). *Singapore: A Case Study in Rapid Development*, IMF Occasional Papers 119, International Monetary Fund.

Boycko, M., A. Shleifer and R. W. Vishny (1996). A theory of privatisation. *Economic Journal*, 106(435), 309–319.

Bozec, R., G. Breton and L. Cote (2002). The performance of state-owned enterprises revisited. *Financial Accountability and Management*, 18, 333–407.

D'Souza, J., R. C. Nash and W. L. Megginson (2001). *Determinants of Performance Improvements in Privatized Firms: The Role of Restructuring and Corporate Governance.* Paper presented at the AFA 2001, New Orleans.

DeWenter, K. L. and P. H. Malatesta (2001). State-owned and privately owned firms: An empirical analysis of profitability, leverage, and labor intensity. *American Economic Review*, 91(1), 320–334.

Donahue, J. D. (1989). *The Privatization Process.* New York: Basic Books.

Economic Review Committee (2002). *Recommendations on Government in Business.* Singapore.

Elson, A. (2008). Sovereign wealth funds and the international monetary system. *Whitehead Journal of Diplomacy and International Relations*, 9(2), 71–82.

Feng, F., Q. Sun and W. H. S. Tong (2004). Do government-linked companies underperform? *Journal of Banking & Finance*, 28(10), 2461–2492.

Lim, C. Y. (1991). *Development and Underdevelopment.* Singapore: Longman.

Lopez de Silanes, F. (1997). Determinants of Privatization Prices. *Quarterly Journal of Economics*, 112(4), 966–1028.

Lyons, G. (2007). State capitalism: The rise of sovereign wealth funds. *Journal of Management Research*, 7(3), 119–146.

Maslakovic, M. (2010). *Sovereign Wealth Funds 2010.* London: International Financial Services London (IFSL).

Megginson, W. L., R. C. Nash and M. van Randenborgh (1994). The financial and operating performance of newly privatized firms: An international empirical analysis. *Journal of Finance*, 49(2), 403–452.

Ministry of Finance. (2002). *Budget Speech 2002.* Retrieved from http://www.mof.gov.sg/budget_2002/economic.html.

Mueller, D. C. (1989). *Public Choice.* Cambridge: Cambridge University Press.

Omar, M. (2007). British withdrawal from Singapore [Electronic Version]. SINGAPORE INFOPEDIA. Retrieved 10 May 2010 from http://infopedia.nl.sg/articles/SIP_1001_2009-02-10.html.

Ow, C. H. (1986). The role of government in economic development: The Singapore experience. In *Singapore: Resources and Growth,* Lim C. Y. and P. Lloyd (eds.), pp. 221–267. Singapore: Oxford University Press.

Ramírez, C. D. and L. H. Tan (2003). *Singapore, Inc. Versus the Private Sector: Are Government-Linked Companies Different*? IMF Working Paper No. 03/156, International Monetary Fund.

Sabhlok, A. (2001). *The Evolution of Singapore Business: A Case Study Approach.* Working Paper, Institute of Policy Studies, Singapore.

Singh, K. and S. H. Ang (1998). *The Strategies and Success of Government Linked Corporations in Singapore.* Research Paper Series #98–06, Faculty of Business Administration, National University of Singapore.

Tan, C. H. (1990). Privatization in Singapore: The success of public sector management. *International Journal of Public Sector Management,* 3(1), 47–57.

Tan, C. H. (1992). Singapore Telecom: From Public Sector to Private Sector. *International Journal of Public Sector Management,* 5(4), 4–14.

Tan, H. (1996). State capitalism, multinational corporations, and Chinese entrepreneurship in Singapore. In *Asian Business Networks,* Hamilton, G. G. (ed.), pp. 157–169. Berlin: Walter de Gruyter.

Temasek Holdings (2009). *Temasek Review 2009.*

Temasek Holdings (2010). *Temasek Report 2010.*

Vining, A. R. and A. E. Boardman (1992). Ownership versus competition: Efficiency in public enterprise. *Public Choice,* 73(2), 205–239.

Yeung, H. W.-C. (2000). State intervention and neoliberalism in the globalizing world economy: Lessons from Singapore's regionalization programme. *The Pacific Review,* 13(1), 133–162.

Chapter 10

GROWTH, OPPORTUNITY, AND INEQUALITY: SOME EMPIRICS FROM SINGAPORE

HO Kong Weng

While the strategy of openness had earned Singapore rapid economic growth, upward social mobility, and possibly decreasing inequality in the early years of development, the more recent years has seen increasing inequality. With this inequality comes an underlying possibly diminished upward inter-generational mobility, due to skill-biased growth processes, skill-biased parental influence, liberalisation in the education industry, and structural changes in the society, which hurt the human capital accumulation of children in families under economic and intra-household stresses. In particular, paternal influence on educational aspirations and attainment is more pronounced than maternal influence. Non-Chinese and youths from disrupted families are worse off in both educational aspirations and educational attainment.

INTRODUCTION

Singapore's economic growth has been spectacular over a period close to five decades, making many developing countries envious of her economic performance. Using 2005 prices, the real gross domestic product (GDP) per person in 2009 was 11.9 times that in

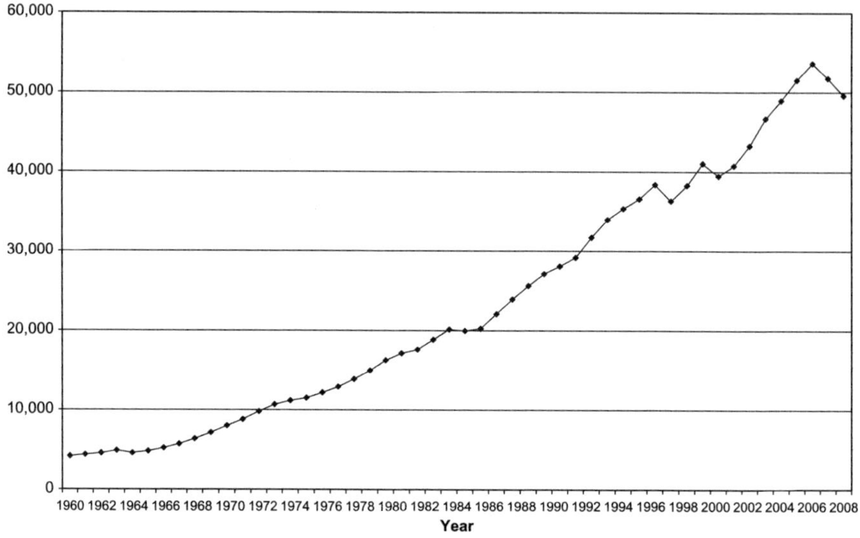

Fig. 1: Per capita real GDP, S$ in 2005 prices.

1960, implying an average real growth rate of 5.3% per annum. Figure 1 depicts the phenomenal growth of the Singapore economy from 1960 till 2009. Although there were some dips during several episodes of recessions, the Singapore economy recovered rather quickly.

Would such a rapid and persistent growth of the Singapore pie translate to opportunities for all? Is the growth process an even one, benefiting the skilled as well as the unskilled? How do the children from the less well-to-do fare? These are some of the questions we want to explore in this chapter.

In this chapter, we simply measure economic growth by the change in real GDP per person over time and propose to measure opportunity by the inverse of the dependence of one's economic status on one's parents. If one's economic status in terms of income, educational attainment, or occupation is highly dependent on parental economic status, then we would say that inter-generational mobility is low, which is equivalently, for our purpose in this chapter, a low level of opportunity in the society. Note that inter-generational mobility or opportunity is a dynamic measure of inequality. One static measure of inequality is the Gini coefficient, which has a value in the range from zero to one. The Gini coefficient has a larger value when the income distribution is more unequal. When income inequality is high, it has two effects at the ground level of the individuals: one positive and the other negative. The positive effect is an incentive for the less-to-do to upgrade via training, educational investment, and searching of opportunity for themselves and their children. The negative effect could be merely psychological such as feeling of being envious of others or of unfairness. But if a high level of inequality is also related to access to resources for investment in physical and human capital so that opportunities in the future can be improved, then inequality will become entrenched and sticky in the sense that there is no opportunity to move from one economic class to another for oneself or for one's children, resulting in social stratification or inter-generational immobility.

How is social mobility or inter-generational mobility measured? Before answering that question, we want to understand an important concept of social mobility: absolute vs. relative mobility. Absolute upward mobility for all is possible, but it is impossible to have relative upward mobility for all as when a person or the person's offspring climbs up the social ladder, another person or this other person's offspring must have slipped down the social ladder. The weights of relative positions in a ranking ladder at a point in time represent the distribution of socioeconomic status. Over time and over generations, changes in the weights of each relative position in a social ladder give a measure of the dynamic changes in the distribution of people in the social ladder, and hence there is exactly why relative social mobility is related to inequality in society. Forces affecting social mobility, which is a dynamic measure across time, will influence how a static measure of inequality will evolve dynamically. Using aggregate data, I examine the extent of social mobility in Singapore; when we have micro data linking generations, I provide the estimates of inter-generational mobility.

I examine a simple demand–supply framework of social mobility and inequality to understand how structural changes in technology, demography, and government policies in education and the labour market may affect the joint equilibrium of social mobility and inequality. In this theoretical model, I define inequality as wage inequality, which is the ratio of skilled wage to unskilled wage. I use this model to investigate how educational liberalisation, population expansion via skill-biased immigration, and family disruption may worsen or improve inequality and social mobility in Singapore.

The rest of the chapter is as follows. Section 2 identifies the main causes of income inequality in Singapore and presents some empirical findings. Section 3 provides a brief survey of existing studies on social mobility in Singapore. Section 4 presents our findings on social mobility in Singapore, using latest available data, and with a focus on inter-generational mobility in education. I present a simple demand–supply framework of upward mobility and wage inequality in Sec. 5. Section 6 discusses the impact of educational liberalisation, population expansion, and rising family disruption. Section 7 concludes the chapter.

CAUSES OF INCOME INEQUALITY IN SINGAPORE

Singapore is a very open society, welcoming foreign investment, imports, foreign talents, as well as foreign unskilled migrant workers. Being open to international forces could be a reason for widening inequality as documented for both advanced and developing countries in the United Nations Development Programme's *Human Development Report* (1999). Furthermore, Taylor (2000) showed that external economic liberalisations of 11 developing countries had surely widened the skilled-unskilled wage gap despite ambiguous impact on economic growth.

On the other hand, globalisation seemed to have aided Singapore in terms of economic growth. Linking herself to a world of advanced ideas, Singapore is able to grow rapidly as a technology follower. Ho and Hoon (2009) showed theoretically in a model and empirically using Singapore data that channels of technology diffusion measured by (a) ratio of stock of G5 foreign direct investment to total capital stock, (b) ratio of imports of machinery and transport equipment from G5 countries to GDP, and (c) quality of learning as in the ratio of tertiary enrolment to employment contribute to the multi-factor productivity growth rate and hence economic growth. While Ho and Hoon (2009) did not examine the impact of advanced ideas transmission on income inequality, we suspect that these channels of global technology diffusion could be skill biased and hence may bring about a growth process accompanied by rising income inequality in Singapore.

Singapore had relied on foreign workers, both skilled and unskilled, even before her independence in 1965 as she was and still is an immigrant society to a certain extent. The locals do not want to take up low-paying manual jobs, and hence an import of unskilled migrant workers is necessary. An inflow of unskilled foreign workers will reduce the upward movement of unskilled wage, if any at all, even with economic growth. On the other hand, there is also a high demand for the scarce high-end skills in Singapore, and the internationally mobile foreign talent will command a world competitive wage which accelerates with economic growth in Singapore and other parts of the world. Furthermore, nonwage or asset income, usually within the portfolio of the skilled but not the unskilled, grows in tandem with economic growth.

Competing for international investment and highly skilled and internationally mobile talents, Singapore has revised the marginal income tax rates and the corporate tax rate over the years, resulting in a possibly less progressive tax structure compared to the past. Such a policy encourages workers to move up the income ladder with the correct incentives but at the same time has a potential adverse impact on income inequality. In Singapore, capital gains are not taxed, and estate duty has been abolished in 2008. The Goods and Services Tax (GST) was introduced in April 1994 at 2%. It had been raised gradually to 7% in June 2008. As a consumption tax, GST is regressive in nature.

Realising the need to assist low-wage workers in Singapore, the Ministerial Committee on Low Wage Workers was set up in 2005 to recommend measures to improve employability and income security for low-wage workers and to help families break out of the poverty cycle. Six spokes of assistance within the Workfare framework were outlined: Rewarding Work; Social Support to Enable Work; Higher Skills for Better Jobs; Expand Job Opportunities; Creating Hope for the Future; and Sharing in the Nation's Progress. The Ministerial Committee on Low Wage Workers (2009) reported on 7 June 2009 that the government had spent over S$1.1b from 2006 to 2008 helping low-wage Singaporeans. As a result, "since 2006, low wage workers have made significant progress in their incomes and availed themselves to job opportunities. The wages of the 20th percentile full-time employed resident increased from $1,200 a month in 2006 to $1,310 in 2008". "In addition, Singapore's income inequality has reduced, as reflected by the drop in Singapore's Gini coefficient from 0.489 in 2007 to 0.481 in 2008, the first decline since 1998. After adjusting for government benefits and taxes, the Gini coefficient drops even further, to 0.462". Our question: Is the drop caused primarily by the recession or the initiatives of the government? It could be a mixture of both and we will be able to answer this question more confidently with a few more years of data in the future.

Based on the discussion above, Ho (2010a) explores a time-series investigation on the Gini coefficient of Singapore. The Gini coefficients are obtained from the World Institute for Development Economics Research (2008) for the earlier years and from Singapore Department of Statistics (2010) for the later years. The results and interpretations are extracted from Ho (2010a) and presented in Table 1.

Regression 1 in Table 1 suggests an inverse Kuznets curve, which is seemingly surprising. Regression 2 highlights the importance of technology transmission channels in influencing income inequality in Singapore, a small open economy in a world of ideas. An increase in G5 foreign ownership of capital in Singapore will lead to an increase in income inequality. Similarly, with more tertiary students relative to employment, a proxy for quality of learning, Gini will increase. Both channels are likened to skill-biased forces which will raise income inequality. Imports of advanced machinery from G5 countries, however, will reduce income inequality. Regression 3 shows that with these channels as controls on the right-hand side, the usual Kuznets curve

Table 1: Determinants of income inequality (Gini).

	(1) Gini	(2) Gini	(3) Gini	(4) Gini
ln(G5 imports of machinery and transport equipment/GDP)		−0.036***	−0.084***	−0.039***
		(0.012)	(0.022)	(0.012)
ln(tertiary enrolment/employment)		0.043***	−0.025	0.041***
		(0.008)	(0.036)	(0.008)
ln(G5 FDI stock/capital stock)		0.047***	0.031*	0.052***
		(0.011)	(0.018)	(0.011)
ln(real GDP per worker)	−1.665***		1.274**	
	(0.281)		(0.514)	
ln(real GDP per worker)^2	0.080***		−0.054**	
	(0.013)		(0.023)	
Growth rate				0.194*
				(0.099)
Growth acceleration				−0.121*
				(0.070)
Constant	9.147***	0.663***	−7.058**	0.656***
	(1.511)	(0.016)	(3.007)	(0.016)
Observations	37	34	34	34
R-squared	0.753	0.846	0.876	0.865

Source: Ho (2010a).
Notes: Standard errors in parentheses. * significant at 10%; ** significant at 5%; *** significant at 1%.

will be revealed. Regression 4 shows an alternative version of the "Kuznets curve" in terms of growth rates. Structural changes while raising growth lead to an increase in income inequality. Accelerated growth beyond the normal growth will, however, reduce income inequality, possibly because more unskilled work hours are demanded.

The results reported in Ho (2010a) suggest the growth process for Singapore as a technology follower is skill biased and could explain the evolution of income inequality in Singapore rather well. In particular, technology diffusion of advanced ideas via foreign direct investment is skill biased, and the quality of learning or the extent of tertiary enrolment relative to employment, which facilitates technology diffusion of advanced ideas, is also skill biased.

However, technology diffusion via imports of advanced machinery is likely to be not skill biased, benefiting the unskilled workers relative to the skilled workers.

PAST STUDIES ON SOCIAL MOBILITY IN SINGAPORE

Studies on social mobility in Singapore were limited, and often used secondary data or a one-time survey as panel data on economic status are not available. The literature review in Ho (2010b) showed that absolute upward mobility had been high in Singapore due to sustained economic growth and rapid expansion of educational opportunities especially for the families at the lower end of the social ladder, implying also high inter-generational mobility in the past. However, parental background remained an important determinant of one's economic status. See, for example, Chiew (1991) and Ko (1991) who used data collected in 1983. Using data based on a 2001 study, Tan (2004) also found an important role of father in transmitting occupational status.

Ng *et al.* (2009) compared Singapore with the US data and found similar inter-generational immobilities. As both countries have similar economic realities, welfare systems, education regimes, labour structures, and high inequalities, the similar results are hence not surprising. To maintain global competitiveness, policy makers of these two countries face the daunting challenge of overcoming immobility and inequality.

Using data from the same Singapore youth survey conducted in 2002 as in Ng *et al.* (2009) who studied income mobility, Ng and Ho (2006), and Ong and Ho (2006) considered inter-generational transmission of educational attainment and occupational attainment respectively. In particular, Ng and Ho (2006) found that youths whose parents are divorced had their educational attainment lowered by 1.8 to 1.9 years worth of schooling. A Swedish study by Jonsson and Gahler (1997) has also demonstrated that children who have experienced family dissolution or reconstitution show lower educational attainment at age 16. A single parent, usually the mother, forced to work outside instead of relying on her husband, will have less time in the supervision of the child in school work. The child is burdened with psychological costs caused by the divorce of his or her parents, leading to lower emotional quotient (EQ) and social quotient (SQ) compared to children from intact families enjoying love and care from both parents.

Can we use principles of economics to explain the transmission of educational status from fathers to their children? Yes, as fathers are usually the breadwinners, their educational attainment will determine usually the amount of income they will earn for their families and children. A highly educated man is also likely to marry a highly educated woman through a process called positive assortative matching. As the price of time of the well-to-do couple is high, they are likely to choose fewer children and invest more in the education of their children relative to couples who are less well-to-do. Consequently, we observe an educational- and skill-biased parental influence on the educational attainment of their children.

Findings from Ong and Ho (2006) on the transmission of occupational status showed that three parental background variables, namely father's education, mother's education, and father's occupation, had stronger indirect effect on job attainment of the youth via influencing educational attainment of the youth than the direct effect on job attainment. The status of parental divorce had strong negative effects, both directly on job attainment and indirectly on the educational attainment of the youth.

Ho (2010b) concluded that absolute upward mobility had been high in the past, but recent studies on income mobility pointed that Singapore could have become less mobile.

NEW EMPIRICS ON SINGAPORE

Using census data and household survey data, at the aggregate level, Ho (2010b) found significant absolute upward mobility in educational attainment as well as in occupational status from 1990 to 2005. The driver of the absolute upward mobility is a rapidly growing Singapore economy, giving more opportunities to educational

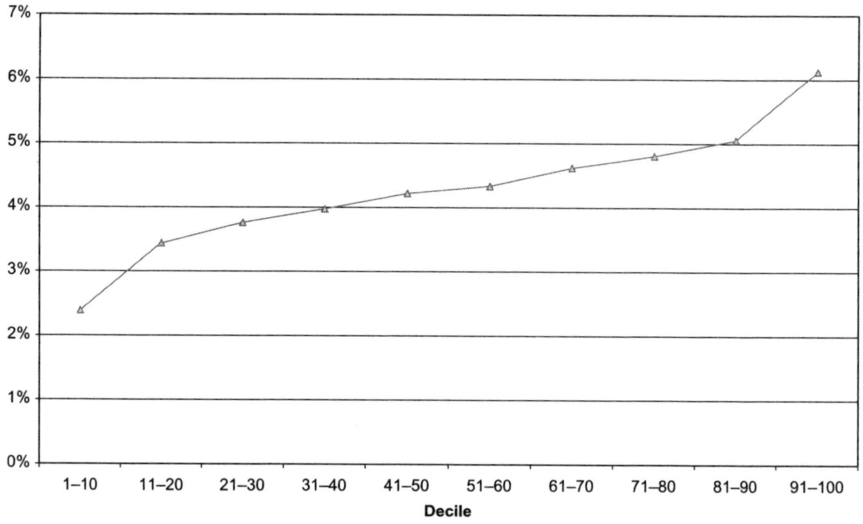

Fig. 2: Nominal annual growth rate of average monthly income from work per household member among employed households by decile from 1995 to 2009.

Notes: Figure 2 has used the latest data to update a similar figure found in Ho (2010b). Nominal values are used because real values are not available from published data from the Government of Singapore.

attainment and occupational upgrading, and reflecting in the distributional change in education and occupation.

How about the distribution of income growth over the years? Figure 2 shows the average nominal growth rate of average monthly income from work per household member among employed households by deciles from 1995 to 2009.[1] Although the growth rates are nominal as real values are not available, if inflation over the same period did not penalise the rich more than the poor, the information on nominal values will remain useful. Household income inequality has worsened as the lower deciles have experienced lower growth rates than the upper deciles. Economic growth in Singapore from 1995 to 2009 had been uneven, benefiting the upper end more

[1] Computation is based on data from Singapore Department of Statistics (2007), (2009), and (2010).

than the lower end. Unfortunately, Fig. 2 does not provide information on the mobility of households across deciles and does not contain information across generations. However, it does suggest that opportunity for the families at the lower end of the social ladder could be diminished. Therefore, it is all the more important to gather data-linking generations systematically for future analysis on income mobility.

Next, I present our analysis using data from the two surveys commissioned by the National Youth Council in 2002 and 2005. The samples were drawn from sampling frames obtained from the Department of Statistics and matched the national youth population by nationality, age, gender, and ethnicity. Reports on the surveys are published in Ho and Yip (2003) and Ho and Chia (2006). Pooling the two samples for our regression analysis, I examine the determinants of the educational aspiration of youth aged 15–18 who are students and the educational attainment of working youth aged 23–29 separately. Missing observations in parental education have been imputed. For brevity, I only report the regression results using log of years of schooling. The detailed findings are available in Ho (2010a). Taken from Ho (2010a), Table 2 reports the impact of an additional per cent of parental schooling on the schooling of the youth.

Regressions (1) and (2) of Table 2 report the determinants of the educational aspirations of students aged 15–18, while regressions (3) and (4) show the results for working youths aged 23–29. The influence of fathers on education aspiration and attainment is more pronounced than the mother. Parental income is an important influence too. Female teenage students are more likely to have higher educational aspirations, but gender has marginal or insignificant influence on educational attainment. Non-Chinese and youths from disrupted families are worse off in both educational aspirations and educational attainment.

The coefficient of paternal or maternal education in the regressions represents an inter-generational persistence in education, or an inverse of inter-generational mobility. A lower coefficient means higher educational opportunity not linked to parental background measured by paternal or maternal education. Once parental income

Table 2: Inter-generational education mobility: log of years of schooling.

	(1) ln(aspiration)	(2) ln(aspiration)	(3) ln(attainment)	(4) ln(attainment)
ln(paternal education)	0.031**	0.046***	0.047***	0.058***
	(0.013)	(0.013)	(0.015)	(0.015)
ln(maternal education)	0.011	0.019*	0.027*	0.034**
	(0.012)	(0.011)	(0.015)	(0.013)
ln(parental income)	0.029***		0.029***	
	(0.007)		(0.011)	
Female	0.025***	0.025***	0.025*	0.026*
	(0.009)	(0.009)	(0.015)	(0.015)
Non-Chinese	−0.057***	−0.067***	−0.134***	−0.142***
	(0.011)	(0.011)	(0.017)	(0.017)
Family disruption	−0.055***	−0.061***	−0.072***	−0.084***
	(0.019)	(0.019)	(0.021)	(0.020)
Year 2005	0.023**	0.020**	0.024	0.024
	(0.010)	(0.010)	(0.015)	(0.015)
Constant	2.358***	2.541***	2.174***	2.361***
	(0.055)	(0.027)	(0.074)	(0.026)
Observations	835	835	1217	1,217
R-squared	0.154	0.132	0.135	0.124

Source: Ho (2010a).

Notes: Standard errors in parentheses. * significant at 10%; ** significant at 5%; *** significant at 1%.

is added on the right-hand side, the persistence coefficient will be reduced or become insignificant, implying a mediating role of parental income. Does that mean economic growth will then increase educational opportunity through the channel of increasing parental income? The answer is exactly opposite if economic growth is uneven, benefiting the well-to-do more than the lower income groups.

DEMAND AND SUPPLY OF SOCIAL MOBILITY

A simple demand–supply framework of social mobility and wage inequality incorporating insights from the findings reported above has been developed in Ho (2010b). I outline the set-up of the model here. Simply assume the price of upward mobility to be wage equality, which is defined as the ratio of unskilled wage to skilled wage. First, consider how parents decide on educational investment in their children. Altruistic parents maximise overall welfare comprising of their own welfare and the future welfare of their children, which is influenced by parental investment on the education of the children. A child is born unskilled but is likely to be converted to become a skilled adult with investment in education. When wage equality is low, the opportunity cost, or price, of educating an unskilled child to become a skilled adult will be low, and the quantity demand of upward mobility will be high, implying a downward sloping demand curve. A decrease in government subsidy to public education, for example, which influences the parental decision on education based on returns to education, will shift the demand curve of upward mobility downward.

Next, I examine the influence of upward mobility on wage equality. When there are more conversions of unskilled children to skilled adults (higher upward mobility), there will be a larger supply of future skilled workers relative to the supply of future unskilled workers, leading to a lower wage inequality or higher wage equality. Hence, the price of upward mobility (defined as wage equality) is positively related to upward mobility, giving an upward-sloping supply curve. Structural changes in technology or conditions in the labour market will shift the supply curve of upward mobility.

The intersection of the demand and supply curves will give the equilibrium levels of upward mobility and wage equality in the society. In the next section, I use the demand–supply framework developed in Ho (2010b) to discuss issues related to the empirical findings and future prospects on inter-generational upward mobility and wage inequality in Singapore. I use the framework to examine the impact on educational inter-generational mobility.

THEORETICAL IMPACT OF POLICIES AND TRENDS

In this section, I examine the impact of the process of educational liberalisation in Singapore, the consequence of population expansion via skilled immigrants, and the implication of potentially rising cases of family disruption in Singapore.

Liberalisation of the Education Industry

A liberalisation process of schools in Singapore began in 1987 when three top-performing boys' secondary schools turned independent, which brought about public criticism over the elitist nature and the high fees charged by the independent schools. Autonomous school status was first granted to six secondary schools in 1994, giving parents and students a wider choice of schools. The integrated programme (IP) was first implemented in 2004, allowing IP schools to skip the "O" level examinations. Currently, there are a total of 13 independent schools, 36 autonomous schools, and 12 IP schools out of 168 secondary schools, 22 junior colleges, or centralised institutes. These "liberalised" schools are academically more selective than other schools, and it would be interesting to examine the family background of students in these schools. If they have parents with higher education and income compared to students in other schools, the liberalisation process would bring about a skill-biased parental influence on education. Local schools compete with one another in some ranking or benchmarking exercises. In a conference on benchmarking for performance in education organised by the World Bank, Ho (2010c) asked if local benchmarking would translate to competition among schools with parental assistance and whether lower inter-generational mobility and higher inequality would also become the consequences despite gains in efficiency.

In the demand–supply framework outlined earlier, given liberalisation in the education industry, the demand curve will then shift down, resulting in a reduced social upward mobility and lower wage equality, which is a result similar to a process of privatisation in education as private schools rely more on the contribution from parents in terms of both time and money.

Population Expansion via Skill-Biased Immigration

Singapore is targeting a larger population of 6.5 millions within the next 20 to 30 years, from the current level of 4.9 millions despite a very low total fertility rate of 1.28 per resident female in 2008.

Hence, the expansion of the population is likely to be facilitated by skill-biased immigration, and as a result, the skill-biased parental influence will be enhanced as the skilled immigrant parents will have an advantage over the existing unskilled parents in the educational investment of their children. This will shift down the demand curve for upward mobility. However, the supply curve for upward mobility will also shift down or pivot clockwise given a skill-biased immigration for two reasons: first, skilled immigrants are more capable of producing children who will become future skilled workers; second, an influx of skilled immigrants will induce an increased demand for skilled jobs, resulting in an increased skill premium in wages. Therefore, the net effect on upward mobility is ambiguous, given a downward shift in the demand curve and a downward shift or clockwise rotation of the supply curve as illustrated in Fig. 3. It is, however, unambiguous that wage equality will be reduced.

Damage of Family Disruption

Figure 4 shows the rising divorce rates in Singapore since 1980. How will a rising trend of family disruption influence social mobility and

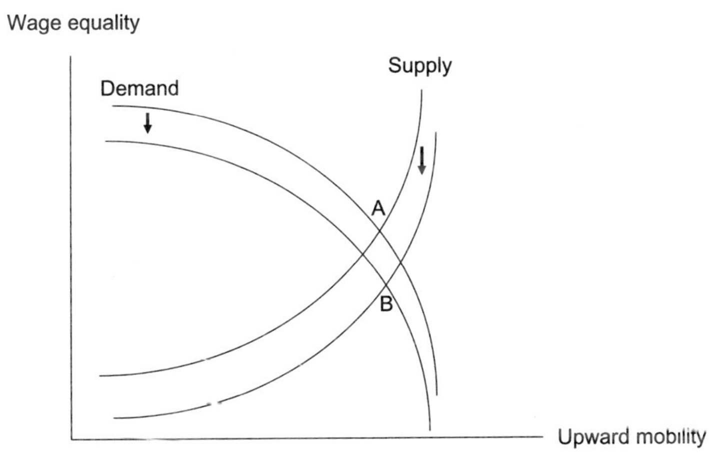

Fig. 3: Skill-biased immigration.

Source: Ho (2010b).

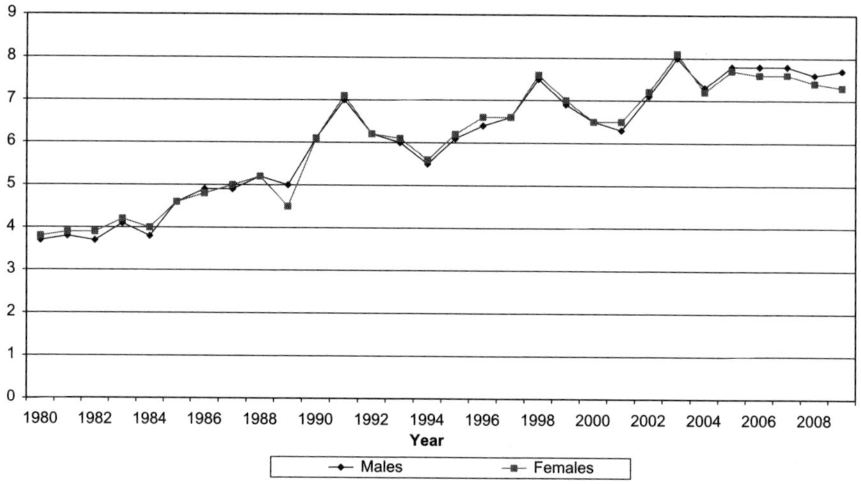

Fig. 4: Gross divorce rate per 1,000 married resident males/females.

inequality? Children from broken families do not receive complete love from both parents. The single parent, likely to be the mother, has to struggle between household production, market activities to bring in the dough, and coaching the child in school work, and as a result, the chances of the child becoming skilled will be reduced, implying a downward shift of the demand curve. Therefore, a rising rate of divorce will bring about lower upward mobility and wage equality. This theoretical result is consistent with the empirical result reported in Table 1.

CONCLUSION

This chapter has collated some empirics on the Singapore economy and found that the strategy of openness had earned Singapore rapid economic growth, upward social mobility, and possibly decreasing inequality in the early years of development. However, the more recent years saw increasing inequality and with it an underlying possibly diminished upward inter-generational mobility due to skill-biased growth processes, skill-biased parental influence, liberalisation in the education industry, and structural changes in the society which hurt the human capital accumulation of children in families under economic and relational stress. While economic growth across the board has increased the economic pie and opportunity for all, whether this channel of social progress will remain an important research and policy question as the nature of economic growth and its benefits have become more unevenly distributed. Furthermore, I suggest that further research be conducted in Singapore on how these macro trends in economic and non-economic variables may have an influence on the well-being of Singaporeans as well as of immigrants living in Singapore.

REFERENCES

Chiew, Seen Kong (1991). Social mobility in Singapore. In *Social Class in Singapore*, Quah, Stella, Seen Kong Chiew, Yiu Chung Ko and Sharon Mengchee Lee (eds.). Singapore: Times Academic Press.

Ho, Kong Chong and Jeffrey Yip (2003). *YOUTH.sg: The State of Youth in Singapore*. Singapore: National Youth Council.

Ho, Kong Chong and Wynne Chia (2006). *YOUTH.sg: The State of Youth in Singapore 2006*. Singapore: National Youth Council.

Ho, Kong Weng (2010a). Inequality of a small and globalized economy in a world of ideas: The case of Singapore. In *Income Inequality: A New Threat to Globalizing Economies*, 10–12 April 2010, Japan: Kyoto Sangyo University.

Ho, Kong Weng (2010b). Social mobility in Singapore. In *Management of Success: Singapore Reassessed*, Chong, Terence (ed.). Singapore: Institute of Southeast Asian Studies.

Ho, Kong Weng (2010c). Educational mobility across generations and inequality: The case of Singapore, *Benchmarking Education Systems for Results: East Asia Regional Conference*, 21–23 June 2010. Singapore: World Bank.

Ho, Kong Weng and Hian Teck Hoon (2009). Growth accounting for a technology follower in a world of ideas: The case of Singapore. *Journal of Asian Economics*, 20(2), 156–173.

Jonsson, Jan O. and Michael Gahler (1997). Family dissolution, family reconstitution, and children's educational careers: Recent evidence of Sweden. *Demography*, 34, 277–293.

Ko, Yiu Chung (1991), Status attainment. In *Social Class in Singapore*, Quah, Stella, Seen Kong Chiew, Yiu Chung Ko and Sharon Mengchee Lee (eds.). Singapore: Times Academic Press.

Ministerial Committee on Low Wage Workers (2009). *Progress Report of Ministerial Committee on Low Wage Workers*. Singapore: Ministry of Manpower.

Ng, Irene, Xiaoyi Shen, and Kong Weng Ho (2009). "Intergenerational earnings mobility in Singapore and the United States. *Journal of Asian Economics*, 20(2), 110–119.

Ng, Regina and Kong Weng Ho (2006). Intergeneration educational mobility in Singapore: An empirical study. *YouthScope*, 1, 58–73.

Ong, Jing Hui and Kong Weng Ho (2006). Intergeneration occupational mobility in Singapore: An empirical study. *YouthScope*, 1, 22–39.

Singapore Department of Statistics (2007). *Key Household Income Trends*, 2006, Occasional Paper on Income Statistics, Vol. February 2007, pp. 1–11.

Singapore Department of Statistics (2009). *Key Household Income Trends*, 2008, Occasional Paper on Income Statistics, Vol. January 2009, pp. 1–10.

Singapore Department of Statistics (2010). *Key Household Income Trends*, 2009, Occasional Paper on Income Statistics, Vol. February 2010, pp. 1–10.

Tan, Ern Ser (2004). *Does Class Matter? Social Stratification and Orientations in Singapore*. Singapore: World Scientific Publisher.

Taylor, L. (2000). *External Liberalization, Economic Performance, and Social Policy*. New York: Oxford University Press.

United Nations Development Programme (1999). *Human Development Report 1999*. New York: Oxford University Press.

World Institute for Development Economics Research (2008). *World Income Inequality Database*. United Nations.

Chapter 11

ARE FINES COMPATIBLE WITH BUILDING A TRULY FINE COUNTRY?

Walter THESEIRA and TAN Di Song

Singapore is a Fine City
$150 — Not Flushing
$1000 — No Urinating in Lifts
$1500 — No Littering
$1000 — No Bird Feeding
$1000 — No Chewing Gum
$1000 — No Spitting
$500 — No Smoking

— popular T-shirt sold on Orchard Road
to tourists visiting Singapore

A fine is a financial penalty imposed on individuals caught breaking one of the many regulations in Singapore governing socially undesirable behaviours. According to standard economic theory, fines increase the relative price of undesirable behaviour, discouraging individuals from choosing such behaviour. However, recent research in behavioural economics suggests that fines may crowd out social norms that intrinsically motivate individuals to behave in socially desirable ways. Consistent with the notion that fines crowd out intrinsic motivation, data from international surveys show that Singaporeans report having relatively low beliefs in individual responsibility and a low level of belief in civic participation. Policy makers should be aware of current research and, before changing policy, should consider carefully whether introducing financial incentives and disincentives may have counterproductive effects on social behaviour.

THE NEOCLASSICAL VIEW: A FINE IS A PRICE, AND EVERYTHING HAS A PRICE

Consider the last time you shopped for groceries, such as rice at the supermarket. How did you make the decision between one brand of rice and another? Perhaps you compared the relative costs of different brands to the relative benefits, the perceived nutritional qualities of each brand. In doing so, you conducted a simple cost–benefit analysis implicitly made in millions of consumer decisions every day. Now, suppose that as you left the supermarket, you bought a drink, finishing it on your way home. How did you make the decision between littering and properly disposing of the empty drink container? If you were rational, you would once again consider the relative costs and benefits. Even the most incorrigible litterbug thinks twice if a policeman is standing before them, while the most upstanding citizen can be tempted to litter if the nearest rubbish bin is an hour away. According to the neoclassical view, if policy makers wish to discourage some types of behaviour, the practical policy is to raise the costs of undesirable behaviour sufficiently to discourage most individuals from doing the "wrong" thing: to not only provide a penalty for proscribed behaviour, but also a reasonable probability of being caught.

To explore this further, consider a simple decision made by thousands of motorists every day in Singapore: whether to pay the correct amount for parking. Payment for parking in many HDB/URA operated car parks is made via prepaid coupons, which have to be displayed according to the time of car park usage. A motorist has a choice: to display a valid number of coupons for the entire length of time parked, or to cheat by displaying less than the required number. In a recent survey conducted by Ong and Theseira (2010), we found that a significant proportion of surveyed motorists would contemplate cheating on car park coupons, and indeed, that many motorists have been fined for parking violations, with some people surveyed having accumulated dozens of fines within the past year. Clearly, cheating on car park coupons is endemic in Singapore. Why this is so, and what can be done about it, can be easily analysed with the basic cost–benefit model of decision making.

The cost–benefit model highlights that the most important predictors of behaviour are the relative costs and benefits facing the decision maker. The benefits of cheating are obvious: the motorist saves money for every coupon not displayed and gets to park for free. The costs of cheating depend on the amount of the fine charged for being caught, and the probability of being detected. A motorist implicitly makes such a cost–benefit calculation when choosing whether to correctly pay for parking; a motorist who sees no parking enforcement officer nearby may be tempted to post-date a coupon by five or 10 minutes or may choose to forgo a coupon entirely. If we treat cheating on car parks as essentially a cost–benefit problem, we can predict that the incidence of cheating should be higher in car parks where the benefits are relatively high, such as around the city centre. The cost–benefit model also provides us with the policy response: High benefits from cheating should be countered by raising the costs from cheating, through increasing the fines for being caught in more expensive parking zones, and/or by increasing enforcement activity in those areas.

More generally, fines are a policy tool for increasing the prices of undesirable behaviours relative to the prices of more desired behaviour. Just as consumers substitute from more expensive goods to less expensive goods when prices rise, so do individuals change their behaviour when the relative prices of different behaviours change. A fine, as a price that we *pay* for choosing "bad" behaviour, operates on the same principle as an incentive, which is a price that we *receive* for choosing "good" behaviour. An incentive implicitly imposes a relative financial penalty — a fine! — on individuals who *do not* change their behaviour. For example, a baby bonus scheme which gives benefits to parents lowers the price of having children relative to the price of not having any children, just as legislating fines for childless people would. From the viewpoint of standard economic theory, fines, discriminatory taxes, and other financial incentives and disincentives are all policy levers that regulate behaviour by altering relative prices.

What justifies the frequent application of fines in public policy in Singapore? A majority of socially undesirable behaviours subject to fines in Singapore are behaviours that generate negative externalities, or costs to third parties, of some type. For example, littering is convenient for the litterbug because he or she does not have to be concerned with searching for a rubbish bin. But littering imposes costs on other parties; litter reduces the value of scenic views and common spaces to others and increases the costs of cleaning and maintenance. Since the litterbug does not bear these costs imposed on other parties, his or her natural tendency will be to litter whenever it is convenient. A fine that is imposed on those caught littering increases the personal cost to the litterbug and helps to align their personal costs from littering (the fine and the probability of being caught) with the social costs of littering. The economic rationale for many other fines in Singapore follows from the basic principle that these proscribed behaviours often impose external costs on others and hence are socially undesirable. Partially, Singapore's success in keeping our city spanking clean can be attributed to appropriately priced and enforced fines.

THE BEHAVIOURAL VIEW: A FINE IS A PRICE, BUT PRICES HAVE UNINTENDED EFFECTS ON BEHAVIOUR

While fines may seem to Singaporeans to be the natural policy tool for regulating behaviour, recent research indicates that the act of formally pricing undesirable behaviour may have unintended negative consequences. Consider the results of a policy experiment conducted by Gneezy and Rustichini (2000b) on childcare centres in Israel. Childcare centres everywhere have the same problem: parents have busy schedules and often arrive late to pick up their children at the end of the day. When parents are late, childcare workers have to stay back late to take care of the children. Clearly, being late in this context is undesirable behaviour. As if inspired by a trip to Singapore, the researchers decided to conduct a policy experiment to impose a fine on parents for being late. Did the incidence of late behaviour fall in response to the increased price of being late, as standard economic theory would predict? The results may surprise you.

Far from reducing late arrivals by parents, introducing fines for being late actually *increased* the incidence of late behaviour. How can we rationalise this counterintuitive finding? While the fine may have increased the *explicit* monetary price for being late, the fine may also have eroded or eliminated the *implicit* non-monetary price for being late. Consider how *you* feel when you are late for an event; you might feel embarrassment, even guilt, if by being late, you have imposed on others. The parents paid an *implicit* price in terms of violating a social norm when they were late for picking up their children. The fine effectively replaced the implicit price of being late, with an explicit price in the form of a fine. The fine transformed the parents' understanding of the act of staying back by the child centre staff, from a social favour to a paid service. Once the option to be late became a paid service, parents with a willingness to pay for the additional time were happy to do so.

To make matters worse, the researchers found that social norms and implicit prices, once eroded by explicit monetary prices, are not easily restored. The researchers concluded their experiment by reverting back to the old, "no fine" policy. But, they found that parents did not revert to their pre-fine social norm of trying to avoid being late: Parents continued being late at about the same rate as under the "fine" policy. The introduction of fines appears to have fundamentally changed the behaviour of parents by weakening the social norms proscribing lateness. Once being late became something parents could pay for, parents found it difficult to go back to considering being late as a social imposition on others. Fines and incentives, by introducing explicit monetary prices to social behaviours, may weaken our ability to follow social norms that would otherwise shape our behaviour.

Nearly four decades ago, in the *The Gift Relationship*, Titmuss (1970) famously argued that the best way to solve the problem of insufficient human blood donations was to rely on purely voluntary donations, rather than contemplate paying for blood, which could erode social values. While economists initially resisted the notion that increasing financial incentives could be counterproductive, more contemporary work provides broad support for the notion that financial incentives fundamentally alter social behaviour in unexpected ways. But what are the mechanisms which drive these results, and can we model them to better shape our thinking about policy? Two recent classes of economic models address these issues. Their common starting point is the observation that individuals often choose personally costly behaviours even when there are no external monetary rewards available, or when the external rewards are insufficient to compensate. For example, military servicemen risk their lives for their country even though their salaries are likely insufficient for the risk (salaries for mercenaries are significantly higher), while many people give blood routinely even though they are not even compensated. How do economic models explain such seemingly selfless behaviours?

The first class of models, drawing from research in psychology and other social sciences and summarised in Frey and Jegen (2001), focuses on the explanation that many social decisions are *intrinsically motivated* in the some way — individuals are responding to an internal motivation rather than external rewards in choosing costly social behaviours. If this view is correct, then the problem with the application of external monetary rewards or punishments is that they have the potential to *crowd out* internal motivations — a problem termed the "hidden cost of reward" (Lepper and Greene, 1978).

Results from research reinforce the point. An experiment by Gneezy and Rustichini (2000a) tasked subjects to answer a series of IQ-test questions. The experimenters varied the amount of compensation offered to subjects for answering questions correctly, ranging from zero compensation to several dollars per correct answer. Standard economic theory predicts that higher compensation should induce greater effort from subjects, and indeed, this basic pattern was found in the data, consistent with real-world field evidence from Lazear (2000). However, subjects who were offered only a token amount — about the equivalent of 30 Singapore cents per correct question — performed *worse* than subjects who were offered nothing at all. Why did this occur? One explanation is that when facing the task without any expectation of reward, subjects were intrinsically motivated to perform well, perhaps because they enjoyed the challenge or wished to prove to themselves that they were smart. The addition of a token reward, far from increasing the incentive to perform well, appears to have displaced these intrinsic motivations in subjects' minds. Indeed, the piece rate of 30 cents per question appears to have been too pitiful to warrant a decent effort from subjects, leading them to give lower levels of effort than they would have given with no monetary reward at all.

Crowd-out effects can be significant for policy makers at the national level. Frey and Oberholzer-Gee (1997) surveyed Swiss households preparing to vote on the undesirable prospect of building a nuclear waste depository in their communal vicinity. About 50.8% of the respondents agreed to the project when no compensation was offered, even though residents were aware of the potential risks of the project and cited these concerns to interviewers. However, when interviewers mentioned monetary compensation, the level of acceptance dropped to 24.6%.[1] Once again, standard economic models predict the opposite: the addition of price incentives ought to increase acceptance rather than decrease it. However, models that incorporate intrinsic motivations would suggest that in an uncompensated, non-monetary environment, residents may be motivated to accept the nuclear waste repository as a civic duty. However, when compensation is offered, the residents view compensation as a price for which they are selling their health. This example demonstrates that intrinsic motivations can be a powerful force for obtaining social compliance and individual acceptance of painful outcomes for the good of the community — so powerful, in fact, that the monetary compensation required to obtain the same level of compliance in a market transaction might be extremely high.

---

[1] The amounts varied from the equivalent of SGD$3,250, SGD$6,525, and SGD$9,785 per person, per year.

The second class of models draws on the observation that many social behaviours are considered admirable or virtuous precisely because these behaviours are not explicitly rewarded by the market. For example, society praises volunteers who donate blood, but often regard with distaste someone who sells their blood for money. Since the same goal is achieved in either case, what matters to society is the *intent* of the blood donor. The difference is that the volunteer is sacrificing without receiving a market reward, providing a *credible signal* of their good intentions. The introduction of monetary incentives erodes the value of the signal, because these "virtuous" social behaviours become relatively less costly to the individual choosing them. If all blood donors are paid generously, one can no longer infer if a donor is a true volunteer or someone selling their blood for money. Benabou and Tirole (2006) provide the foundations for this class of models by introducing signalling concerns, along with the standard price effects caused by incentives, into the model. Thus, a monetary incentive would increase the desired behaviour only if the value of the monetary gain is greater than the harm caused by the loss in value of the signal.

Evidence supports the Benabou and Tirole model of signalling as a motivation for social behaviour. Mellstrom and Johannesson (2008) asked Swedish students to donate blood, dividing students into three treatment groups. The first treatment group was not paid, the second was offered the equivalent of SGD $10,[2] and the third was offered a choice between payment of SGD $10 and donating the money to a charity. In their sample, the number of female students willing to donate blood dropped by almost half, compared to the no-payment group, when students were offered direct cash payment. By contrast, when students were offered cash payments that could be donated directly to charity, there was no drop-off in donation rates, perhaps because the signalling value of having donated blood was the same. Ariely *et al.* (2009) provide more evidence in their experiment "Clicking for Charity". Participants could generate donations

[2] Original amounts were paid in Swedish Krona.

to the Red Cross by clicking two keys on a keyboard; a higher number of clicks, while requiring more effort from the participant, generated a larger donation to charity. They found that participants who were asked to reveal their performance in public put in significantly more effort than participants who could keep their performance private. In addition, introducing cash payments for greater effort led to increased effort for participants who kept their performance private, but did not appear to increase effort in participants who had to disclose their performance in public. The significant increase in private effort after introducing monetary incentives provides more support for a signalling-based explanation of behaviour here, instead of an intrinsic motivation-based explanation; we should not expect intrinsic motivation to be affected differently by payments, regardless of whether the participants' behaviour was visible.

THE SINGAPORE CONTEXT: COULD FINES ERODE THE SOCIAL BASIS FOR A FINE CITY?

The implication from recent research is that policy makers should tread carefully when targeting behaviours which are ordinarily governed by strong social norms or social consensus, especially if intending to alter relative prices through financial incentives or disincentives. Consider the problem of human organ transplantation and donation, which is plagued by continual shortages. While classical economics would have justified using explicit financial prices to clear the market, economists today should also acknowledge current research that suggests pricing human organs and otherwise introducing monetary incentives and disincentives may have significant counterproductive effects on voluntary donations and compliance. Relative prices are deceptively easy to adjust, but may result in consequences that are difficult to predict.

Residents and visitors alike to Singapore can plainly see that public policy widely uses fines to discourage socially undesirable behaviour. Arguably, these fines have worked, in the sense that fines have helped Singapore resolve many problems that are endemic to most urban areas, such as littering and unhygienic behaviour.[3] But has the widespread use of fines crowded out social norms regarding civic duty and communal responsibility that would have otherwise motivated Singaporeans to keep the city clean, green, and gracious? Determining whether the act of using fines directly causes a reduction in social norms supporting good behaviour or civic mindedness is beyond the scope of this chapter. However, we document that in a range of survey evidence, Singaporeans report themselves to have a comparatively weaker sense of civic duty and individual responsibility than citizens of many other countries. This pattern of responses is consistent with the notion that in Singapore today, the social norms favouring intrinsically motivated social behaviour may be relatively weak.

The bulk of the data is from the World Values Survey (WVS) which periodically surveys people around the world a wide range of questions to obtain their views on political, economic, and moral issues. We selected questions from the WVS that may shed light on the view of Singaporeans on social values relating to intrinsic motivation. If the behavioural view were correct, we would predict that the strength of Singaporeans' beliefs in personal responsibility, self-regulation, and civic duty would decrease as fines increase, since higher fines crowd out intrinsic motivation and replace it with extrinsic motivation stemming from financial disincentives. To test this hypothesis, we need to observe Singaporeans' responses over a period of time so we can match changes in attitudes to changes in local fine levels. However, Singapore was surveyed only once in WVS 2002, so we lack variation over time that would help us identify the relationship between motivation and fines. Our second-best option is to compare Singapore's survey responses with societies similar to Singapore except with different fine rates to observe if differences

[3] This statement is an open empirical question. To our knowledge, there is little published empirical evidence on the causal effect of fines on social behaviour such as littering. The standards for casual proof are high, so a statistics documenting a fall in littering after the introduction of a fine would be suggestive, but not conclusive, for example.

in social norms are correlated with differences in fine rates.[4] Of course, we could not attribute differences in social norms between countries entirely to the differences in fines. With those caveats in mind, a striking picture emerges of a Singapore whose citizens appear to report remarkably low levels of belief in personal responsibility and civic engagement — evidence that is consistent with the behavioural prediction of motivational crowd-out.

The first piece of evidence comes from a survey question on the respondent's ideal society, shown in Table 1. Those surveyed were asked whether they preferred a more regulated society or a more deregulated society reliant on personal responsibility. We limit the sample countries to all Southeast and East Asian countries surveyed with this question[5] to get an Asian perspective on this issue. We can see that besides China which is also tightly regulated, Singapore has

Table 1: Which type of society do you think this country should aim to be in the future?
First statement: A society that assures safety and stability through appropriate regulations *vs.*
Second statement: A deregulated society where people are responsible for their own actions.

Country	First (%)	Somewhat closer to first (%)	Cannot say (%)	Somewhat closer to second (%)	Second (%)
China	81.9	12.3	2.5	1.4	1.9
Singapore	58.8	26.1	7.5	5.8	1.8
Vietnam	49.0	12.4	10.0	6.8	21.8
Philippines	33.5	30.2	23.8	8.3	4.3
Japan	10.9	26.3	29.4	25.1	8.2

Source: World Values Survey, various years.

[4] This is practically impossible because two countries often differ in many aspects other then fine levels. Though if we lower our expectations to find suggestive evidence instead, then perhaps an acceptable comparison is between loosely similar countries, like between Asian countries.

[5] Not all countries were asked the same questions.

the least percentage of respondents inclined towards a society based on personal responsibility[6] at 7.6% compared to Japan at 33.3%, Philippines at 12.6%, and Vietnam at 28.6%. One interpretation is that Singaporeans have low motivation to take personal responsibility, even when asked to consider what kind of society they wish to work towards in the future — consistent with the notion that high levels of policy regulation through fines are crowding out intrinsic motivation.

In the next comparison, we consider responses from a wide set of countries on the respondent's preferences between government vs. personal responsibility for the provision of social welfare. Specifically, respondents were asked to report on a scale of 1 to 10 whether they agreed more closely with the statement "People should take more responsibility to provide for themselves" or with the statement "The government should take more responsibility to ensure that everyone is provided for." One is defined as complete agreement with the first statement on government provision, while 10 is complete agreement with the second statement on personal responsibility. To conveniently summarise the results, we sum up the percentage of people who responded with values one to five for each country. The resulting statistic can then be interpreted as the percentage of people who are more inclined towards personal responsibility, and away from government responsibility. A lower percentage value would mean a lower regard for personal responsibility, and a heavier reliance on governmental providence.

The WVS surveyed 79 countries with this question, and of those countries Armenia had the lowest percentage of respondents inclined towards personal responsibility, at 19.7%, while Switzerland had the highest at 82.7%. The average percentage value is 46.64%, and Russia had the median value of 45.3%. Singapore slots in at 42.5%, slightly below both the average and the median.

Before interpreting the results, we note that this question does not ask for the respondent's vision of an ideal society, unlike the

[6] Inclining towards social responsibility is defined as those who answered "somewhat closer to second" and "second."

earlier question, but rather asks how society should change relative to the present. It is possible that even citizens who believe in an ideal society based on personal responsibility could respond that they desire more government provision relative to the current situation, not because they want to avoid responsibility, but because the current government may be incompetent. Poorer countries are more likely to have difficulty providing for the basic infrastructure — roads, power, education, courts, etc. — to allow citizens to engage in productive market activities and make a living for themselves. Therefore, responses from these countries might significantly understate their citizens' true regard for personal responsibility.

Keeping the above in mind, we reduce the sample to 30 countries defined as "Advanced Economies" by the International Monetary Fund.[7] These countries are "advanced" in terms of their economic output and hence are materially prosperous nations. This subsample significantly diminishes the problem of countries reporting lower percentage values because of unmet material needs, instead of lower intrinsic motivation. In Table 2, we rank the 30 countries from the lowest "percentage who responded with values one to five" to the highest. In this reduced sample, the average and median values are 58.2 and 62.0% respectively. Here Singapore ranks the 6th lowest among advanced countries, about 16% lower than the average value. The below-average regard of Singaporean respondents for personal responsibility suggests that most Singaporeans want the government to take care of the problems of social provision and welfare rather than to take care of problems themselves as individuals. This result is especially interesting given that many Western countries in the sample report much stronger beliefs in personal responsibility, relative to Singaporeans — even though Singaporeans often believe that Western countries have stronger public support for government social welfare programs than Singaporeans do. To the extent that an intrinsically motivated member of society would report more desire for personal responsibility, this result again suggests that

[7] There are 33 countries grouped as advanced economies by the IMF, but we could not get WVS data for Cyprus, Israel, and Hong Kong.

Table 2: How would you place your views on a scale of 1 to 10?
1: Complete agreement with "People should take more responsibility to provide for themselves" and
10: Complete agreement with "The Government should take more responsibility to ensure that everyone is provided for".

Rank	Country	Percentage who responded with values 1–5
1	South Korea	13.9
2	Spain	21.8
3	Slovenia	29.6
4	Japan	31.8
5	Slovakia	41.7
6	Singapore	42.5
7	Taiwan	49.3
8	Norway	49.6
9	Greece	51.9
10	Italy	52.2
11	Australia	56.5
12	New Zealand	57.7
13	Malta	57.8
14	Belgium	58.3
15	Canada	61.9
16	Czech Republic	62.0
17	Portugal	64.3
18	Finland	64.9
19	Iceland	65.9
20	The Netherlands	65.9
21	Ireland	68.3
22	The USA	69.4
23	UK	71.1
24	Sweden	73.9
25	Luxembourg	73.5
26	Denmark	76.5
27	Germany	76.7
28	France	76.9
29	Austria	77.2
30	Switzerland	82.7

Source: World Values Survey, various years.

Table 3: Do you agree with this statement? A citizen who does not actively participate in the affairs of his local and national community is not performing his duties.

	Singapore (%)	Taiwan (%)	Philippines (%)	Indonesia (%)	China (%)	Thailand (%)	Mongolia (%)	Vietnam (%)
Agree	35.9	43.6	48.8	56.7	70.5	81.3	84.6	88.5
Disagree	64.1	56.4	51.2	33.0	29.5	18.6	13.6	11.5

Source: East Asian Barometer Survey.

Singaporeans have significantly lesser intrinsic motivation compared to their peers in the richer economies.

The last piece of evidence comes from the East Asia Barometer survey, which is similar in scope to the WVS, but restricts the sample to East Asian countries. We focus on the notion of civic responsibility and attitudes towards civic participation. As shown in Table 3, respondents were asked if they agreed with the statement that "A citizen who does not actively participate in the affairs of his local and national community is not performing his duties." We believe this question directly asks respondents if civic participation is considered a duty. Civic participation and engagement, whether it means attending resident meetings, neighbourhood events, or grassroots volunteering, is seldom required by legislation. Voluntary civic participation relies heavily on an individuals' intrinsic motivation to contribute to their community. Among the sampled countries, Singapore has the lowest percentage of respondents, 35.90%, who agree that active civic participation is a citizen's duty. We argue this implies that Singaporeans have relatively weaker intrinsic motivation when it comes to civic matters.

However, the story does not end there. If extrinsic control over social behaviour crowds out intrinsic motivation, we would expect to see a correlation between the extent of extrinsic control, and the resulting level of intrinsic motivation, across countries. We should find that countries with relatively higher levels of fines should have lower reported intrinsic motivation for civic matters. Using data on the purchasing-power-adjusted fine rates for littering in several

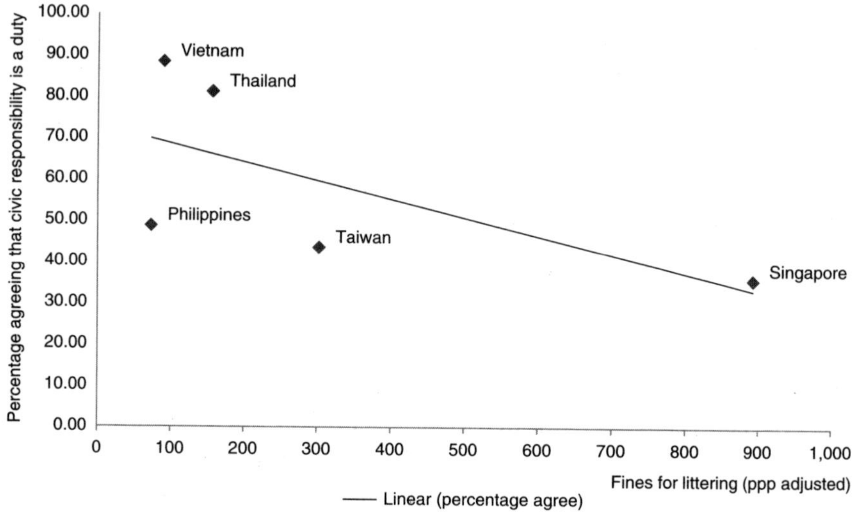

Fig. 1: Negative correlation between fines for littering (PPP) and beliefs in civic responsibility.

Source: East Asian Barometer Survey; Author's calculations from published legislated fines data.

Asian countries (excluding Indonesia, China, and Mongolia due to data constraints), we plot the percentage who agreed with the civic participation statement against the fine rates for littering in these countries to generate Fig. 1.

Note the downward best-fit linear trend in the data, suggesting a negative correlation between the level of fines in a country and the sense of civic responsibility in the country. Higher fines are correlated with a lower degree of intrinsic motivation. This relationship is consistent with the growing body of evidence from the behavioural economics literature that shows increasing external sources of behavioural motivation such as financial incentives and disincentives may reduce intrinsic motivations like civic responsibility.

CONCLUSION

The evidence we have presented suggests that Singaporeans, in a variety of international surveys, report themselves to have relatively low levels of intrinsic motivation. While rigorously attributing a cause for this low level of intrinsic motivation is beyond the scope of this article, recent research in behavioural economics suggests that a high reliance on financial incentives and disincentives as a policy tool may significantly weaken social norms and intrinsic motivation.[8] The first generation of social policies in Singapore made heavy use of financial levers and enforcement. While the successes of that first generation of policy are self-evident everywhere we look in our clean and green country, there may be hidden costs that we have yet to fully recognise. As a new generation of policy makers and citizens come together to build the Singapore of tomorrow, we believe that the time is opportune to revisit policy making in Singapore, and to consider seriously the question whether fines are, in some sense, incompatible with a truly fine country.

REFERENCES

Ariely, Dan, Anat Bracha and Stephan Meier (2009). Doing good or doing well? Image motivation and monetary incentives in behaving prosocially. *American Economic Review*, 99(1), 544–555.

Bénabou, Roland and Jean Tirole (2006). Incentives and prosocial behaviour. *American Economic Review*, 96(5), 1652–1678.

Frey, Bruno S. and Felix Oberholzer-Gee (1997). The cost of price incentives: An empirical analysis of motivation crowding-out. *American Economic Review*, 87(4), 746–755.

Frey, Bruno S. and Jegen Reto (2001). Motivation crowding theory. *Journal of Economic Surveys*, 15(5), 589–611.

Gneezy, Uri and Aldo Rustichini (2000a). A Fine is a Price. *Journal of Legal Studies*, 29(1), 1–18.

Gneezy, Uri and Aldo Rustichini (2000b). Pay enough, or don't pay at all. *Quarterly Journal of Economics*, 115(3), 791–810.

---

[8] We encourage anyone interested to pick up the baton and conduct a rigorous inquiry into whether this erosion of intrinsic motivation is indeed caused by high levels of fines.

Lazear, Edward P. (2000). Performance, pay and productivity. *American Economic Review*, 90(5), 1346–1361.

Lepper, Mark R. and David Green (eds.) (1978). *The Hidden Costs of Reward: New Perspectives on Psychology of Human Motivation*. Hillsdale, NY: Erlbaum.

Mellstrom, Carl and Magnus Johannesson (2008). Crowding out in blood donation: Was Titmuss right? *Journal of the European Economic Association*, 6(4): 845–863.

Ong, Qiyan and Walter Theseira (2010). Waste, sunk cost, and parking: Behavioural biases in motorists' decision making under risk and uncertainty. *Mimeo.*

Titmuss, Richard M. (1970). *The Gift Relationship*. London: Allen and Unwin.

INDEX